ABSOLUTE BEGINNER'S GUIDE

TO

Podcasting

George Colombo
Curtis Franklin Jr.

800 East 96th Street,
Indianapolis, Indiana 46240

Absolute Beginner's Guide to Podcasting

International Standard Book Number: 0-7897-3455-9

Library of Congress Catalog Card Number: 2005929930

Printed in the United States of America

Third Printing: July 2006

08   07   06   4   3

Trademarks

Warning and Disclaimer

Bulk Sales

Que Publishing offers excellent discounts on this book when ordered in quantity for bulk purchases or special sales. For more information, please contact

U.S. Corporate and Government Sales
1-800-382-3419
corpsales@pearsontechgroup.com

For sales outside of the U.S., please contact

International Sales
international@pearsoned.com

Associate Publisher
Greg Wiegand

Acquisitions Editor
Todd Green

Development Editor
Kevin Howard

Managing Editor
Charlotte Clapp

Project Editor
Andy Beaster

Production Editor
Benjamin Berg

Indexer
Ken Johnson

Technical Editors
Jonathan Brown
Dan Brentwood
Eric Rice

Publishing Coordinator
Sharry Gregory

Interior Designer
Anne Jones

Cover Designer
Dan Armstrong

Page Layout
Nonie Ratcliff

Contents at a Glance

Table of Contents

About the Authors

George Colombo has a well-deserved reputation for making technology topics accessible to general audiences. His book *Sales Force Automation* was published in 1993, and many industry observers consider it the starting point for today's multi-billion dollar customer relationship management industry. George has written for a number of business and computer industry publications, including *Computer Reseller News*, *VARBusiness*, *Selling*, and *Sales and Marketing Management*. George spent two years as the host of TEN-TV's *Spotlight Microsoft*, a weekly television show for Microsoft developers. George was also the executive producer for *Conversations with Industry Innovators*, an audio interview series he produced for IBM. He produces podcasts at UltimatePodcasting.com (the companion website for this book) and ProgressiveOrlando.com.

Curtis Franklin, Jr. has been introducing new products and technologies to readers for nearly 20 years. He was the founder of the BYTE Testing Lab for *BYTE* magazine, and since then has written about leading-edge technologies and their impact on individuals and organizations for publications such as *Circuit Cellar INK*, *VARBusiness*, *Solutions Integrator*, ITWorld.com, HowStuffWorks.com, *InternetWeek*, *InfoWorld*, *Network World*, *Secure Enterprise*, and *Network Computing*. As director of labs for Client/Server Labs, he directed testing and analysis of performance, capacity, and capabilities testing for a client list that included IBM, Dell, Microsoft, Intel, Shell Oil, and Blue Cross/Blue Shield of Florida. Today, Curtis directs podcasting strategy and production for TechWeb.com, contributes to security coverage as senior technology editor at *Network Computing*, and edits the Security Channel of TechWeb.com.

Dedication

From George:

—*To Sandy. You're the love of my life.*

From Curt:

—*For Carol, my love and inspiration, and for Daniel, who has taught me more than he can imagine.*

Acknowledgements

From George:

Anthony Colombo provided an expert eye and invaluable suggestions as my part of this manuscript developed, and Joseph Colombo provided the daily prodding I needed to get the job done. I couldn't have written this book without their help and support. Special thanks to Jim Jeter, who helped me flesh out some of the original ideas about how to approach this book. I also want to thank Alicia Rivas for providing important insight into the principles behind great radio and candid input about the book and our podcasts.

When I began this project, radio guru Walter Sabo got me started in the right direction with his unique and authoritative take on radio and podcasting. I'm also indebted to David Brown, Jonathan Brown, Matt Thompson, and Paul Figgiani for their major contributions to this book and to my understanding of podcasting and audio. Thanks to David Fugate for his efforts in finding a home for this book. I was lucky to get to know Tim Bourquin during this project and appreciated his overall support. Finally, let me give an enormous thank you to Todd Green, who has been unbelievably engaged, understanding, and supportive throughout this entire project.

From Curt:

Thanks to George for having the idea for this book, and for inviting me to join him. John Sawyer and Jordan Wiens are young men who dazzle me with their knowledge and skill; I'm grateful that they share both with me on a regular basis. Thanks to Steve Antonoff for late-night IM help sessions, and to Brian Chee for so generously sharing from his vast knowledge of networking and security. I am grateful to Rob Preston, Mike Lee, and my colleagues at *Network Computing* for encouraging me to work on this book. Finally, a much-belated thank you to Mrs. Billie Bryan of Weaver High School, who first taught me to find joy in working with words.

We Want to Hear from You!

As the reader of this book, *you* are our most important critic and commentator. We value your opinion and want to know what we're doing right, what we could do better, what areas you'd like to see us publish in, and any other words of wisdom you're willing to pass our way.

As an associate publisher for Que, I welcome your comments. You can email or write me directly to let me know what you did or didn't like about this book—as well as what we can do to make our books better.

Please note that I cannot help you with technical problems related to the topic of this book. We do have a User Services group, however, where I will forward specific technical questions related to the book.

When you write, please be sure to include this book's title and author as well as your name, email address, and phone number. I will carefully review your comments and share them with the author and editors who worked on the book.

Email: feedback@quepublishing.com

Mail: Greg Wiegand
           Associate Publisher
           Que Publishing
           800 East 96th Street
           Indianapolis, IN 46240 USA

For more information about this book or another Que title, visit our website at www.quepublishing.com. Type the ISBN (excluding hyphens) or the title of a book in the Search field to find the page you're looking for.

Foreword

Welcome to the world of podcasting! From this point on, sleep will seem like a distant memory, caffeine-enhanced drinks will be your crutch, and your relatives will have no idea what you are doing! My name is Rob and I host podCast411. On my podcast, I interview the industry's most successful podcasters to explore what they're doing and why they're successful. Senator John Edwards, Adam Curry, Dawn & Drew, Skepticality, and Wichita Rutherford are just a few of the podcasters I've interviewed.

George Colombo and Curt Franklin asked me to write the foreword for this book, and it's the first foreword I've ever written. When you've never done something before, it can be a bit daunting. Since you are reading this book, I'm going to assume that you are getting ready to create your first podcast...and that probably seems daunting, too. Rest assured, though, that with the help of this book, creating your first podcast will be easier than you think.

Before you start digging into this book, you should ask yourself what type of podcast you want to create. What are you passionate about? What do you want to share with your listeners? There is really no limit to what you can do with your podcast. There are podcasts about the local weather (Kansas City Weather podcast), there are podcasts on Poker (Phil Gordon's World Series of Poker Podcast), there are hundreds of podcasts that play music (see http://music.podshow.com), and there are podcasts just for family and friends. (One couple podcasted all the details of their wedding, up to and including the ceremony. Luckily, they cut it off before the honeymoon!) There are podcasts about *Star Wars* (The Force.net) and about food (Eatfeed). Some podcasts are created by teachers to help educate students or other teachers (The Tech Teachers), while others use podcasts to help fight poverty (Senator John Edwards). The point is that your podcast can be about anything—but it is highly recommended it be about something you care about deeply (as is the case with all the podcasts mentioned previously). Podcasting is a lot of work—make no mistake about that. But it's work you will love doing IF the subject of your podcast is something you are passionate about.

And don't let the microphone intimidate you: If you can write about a subject or even just talk about it, you can podcast on it just as successfully.

Some people in traditional media claim that podcasting is a FAD. If they mean Free Audio Download, then I certainly have to agree. However, if they mean that podcasting is a flash in the pan, then I must disagree with every fiber of my being. They thought that blogging was a fad also, and now there are more than seven million bloggers. A little less than a year ago, there were less than 20 hits when you Googled the term "podcast." Now there are almost 20 million results! This is even more amazing when you consider the fact that there are still fewer than 7,000 podcasters. I predict that the number of podcasters will increase to more than 100,000 within a couple of years and eventually will get close to the one million mark. The time to start podcasting is now, regardless of when you're reading this. Podcasting will be with us for many, many years to come.

So stop wasting time reading this foreword and dig into the meat of this book. And, oh yeah: If your podcast is good enough maybe I'll be interviewing you one of these days!

—Rob, Host, podCast411

INTRODUCTION

Welcome to Podcasting

Once in a while, something comes along that changes the way we think about communicating between people and groups. Desktop publishing did this in the 1980s, and the World Wide Web did it in the 1990s. Here in the first decade of the new millennium, *podcasting*—recorded programs distributed over the Internet and listened to on MP3 players such as the Apple iPod—may well be one of these important "somethings."

In this book, we're going to teach you how to make a successful podcast happen, from planning through syndication, packaging, and marketing. We'll be taking a hands-on approach, walking you through the process of recording and editing a program, bundling it up for others to see, and then doing the web-based work necessary to send it flying out to your waiting public.

Now, after that talk about being hands-on, you'll notice that we spend some time talking about planning before we have you sit down in front of the microphone. The big reason for this is that we've found planning to be the key to reaching the end of the process with a podcast you're happy with. For most of us, keeping track of recording issues and staring at a microphone will be enough of a challenge without having to simultaneously figure out what we're going to talk about. Even when spontaneity and fun are the goals (and why shouldn't they be?), having a rough game plan will make everything much easier.

The good news for all of us is that, with a few very basic tools and techniques in hand, creating a good podcast is pretty darned easy. The odds are pretty good that you already have most of the pieces you need to get started, and coming up with the pieces to fill in the blanks should be simple and inexpensive. In this book, we'll tell you where these very basic pieces will serve you throughout your podcasting career, and where it makes sense to spend a little more money to get a much greater impact.

We're also going to talk about some of the techniques that radio personalities and recording engineers have known about for years—the basic "tricks" that will let you control how your podcast sounds and eliminate most of the "amateur" mistakes that can distract listeners from the most important aspect of your podcast—the content.

MP3 players are ultraportable, and we'll teach you how to take your podcast into the field, so your listeners can follow along as you go to events, look for wildlife, or meet interesting folks on the street. After you've recorded your podcast and edited it into the form you're happy with, we'll teach you how to package it up with the various bits of text and other information listeners will need when they want to find the file. We'll talk about how to get files onto a server, what syndication is all about, and what you'll want the website on which your podcast lives to look like.

Once you start podcasting, you'll be creating intellectual property, so we'll talk about both sides of this issue—how to protect the rights to your intellectual property while respecting the rights of others. Now, we're not giving legal advice, but we will point you at key resources and share some of the generally accepted rules on using and protecting creative works.

Most people will see podcasting as an interesting hobby, but some folks are interested in going beyond a hobby and learning how to make money in podcasting, or use podcasting for their business. We'll look at the issues you'll face as you work with advertisers, sponsors, and subscribers. Finally, we'll share a list of some popular and influential podcasts so you can go out and hear what other podcasters are doing in their recordings.

Whether you want to make a podcast that's funny or dramatic, serious or frivolous, profitable or just for fun, you're going to see that it's easy to build a podcast that introduces listeners you've never met to the sound of your voice and the force of your ideas. It's going to be fun—let's get started.

PART I

THE BASICS

1

AN OVERVIEW OF PODCASTING

Podcasting is an easy and inexpensive method for creating radio-like content that can then be distributed over the Internet. It provides you, as a content creator (that is, podcaster), with capabilities that were previously available only to professional broadcasters and required prohibitively expensive tools.

Podcasting also provides your listeners with a listening experience that has several important advantages over what they get with traditional radio.

IPODS AREN'T NECESSARY

The term podcasting is a *portmanteau*, or a "new word that's formed by joining two others and combining their meanings." (WordNet 2.0, © 2003 Princeton University.) The two words in this case are "iPod," referring to Apple's popular portable music player, and "broadcasting." The term is something of a misnomer, however, insofar as podcasting does not require an iPod. Any portable music player will do quite nicely or, in a pinch, a podcast can be listened to on a computer. In fact, there is a lively, ongoing debate within the podcasting community about whether or not the term is going to stick. In the absence of a good alternative, though, it looks as though it's going to be with us for the foreseeable future.

Podcasting Is Radio As You've Always Loved It— Only Better

If you're old enough to drive, you probably have an intimate relationship with radio.

As is the case with most intimate relationships, this means that radio plays an important part in your everyday life. It is often the first thing you hear when you wake up in the morning, preparing you for the day ahead. You bring it along with you as you drive to work for news and companionship, and it's there with you for the ride home in the evening. It can provide a steady, reassuring presence as you go about your business during the day or it can challenge you with ideas and information that you won't hear anywhere else.

Like other intimate relationships, there are certain things about radio you love but there are also a few things that can be frustrating and annoying. Some radio personalities make you laugh and seem as comfortable and familiar as your favorite uncle. Other on-air personalities can be so infuriating that you actually find yourself screaming at the top of your lungs, eliciting curious stares from people in the car next to you at a red light.

Beyond the obvious love/hate aspects of the relationship, there's another reaction you've probably had more than once while listening to the radio: You've thought to yourself, "I can do that!" It might have happened while you were listening to your favorite taskmaster rant about the news of the day or while your local afternoon drive DJ smoothly announced artists and song titles. You listened and thought wistfully about how much fun it would be to actually be the person behind the microphone for once. Of course, unless you were ready to quit your job and pursue a career in radio, that particular dream was unlikely to ever come true. At least, that was the case before several previously unrelated technologies came together in a perfect high-tech storm and created a genuine grassroots phenomenon known as podcasting.

PODCASTING'S GRASSROOTS ORIGINS

Podcasting didn't emerge from Redmond, Washington or Silicon Valley, and its explosive growth wasn't spurred along by a multimillion dollar marketing campaign. Instead, podcasting was cobbled together from several "off-the-shelf" technologies by small group of technophiles, led by former disc jockey and MTV VJ Adam Curry and programming guru Dave Winer. The earliest known podcast began to appear in late 2004, and by early 2005 thousands of people were posting their podcasts on the Internet. Podcasts emerged that reflected almost every format that radio had ever produced during its long history, along with several formats that radio never dreamed of—or, if it did, never dared to broadcast!

How Podcasting Works

With podcasting, you can turn your desire to get behind a microphone into reality quickly, easily, and inexpensively. But the benefits of podcasting aren't confined to podcasters. In fact, podcasting offers some real advantages for your listeners, too.

A simple definition of podcasting is "a combination of technologies that allows users to create radio-like content with their computers and allows listeners to automatically receive that content over the Internet, then play it on their computers or portable music players."

Let's begin our look at podcasting with an overview of the entire podcasting process. Following the components of our definition, we'll take a look at the basic steps involved in creating a podcast. (Of course, we'll be reviewing the entire process in much greater detail throughout the rest of the book.) Then, we'll examine the elements of your listener's experience, comparing and contrasting it with the experience of listening to traditional radio. Finally, we'll explore the single most important element that differentiates podcasts from traditional radio broadcasts.

The Basic Steps for Creating a Podcast

Podcasters use a wide range of different tools and techniques to put their shows together. Still, there are certain basic steps involved in creating a podcast that are common among all podcasters.

Plan Your Podcast

Of all the steps involved in creating a quality podcast, this is one of the most important. (It's so important, in fact, that Chapter 4 of this book,"Strategies For Planning Each Show," is devoted exclusively to strategies and tactics for effectively planning your podcast.) Incredibly, however, this crucial step receives very little attention in most discussions of podcasting. As a result, many prospective podcasters falter in their efforts because they neglect to spend sufficient time on "show prep." The most successful podcasters make their shows seem effortless, but don't be fooled. An engaging podcast is invariably the product of careful planning and preparation.

Record Your Podcast

Of course, this is the part of the process that's the most fun! This is where you preserve your content—interviews, music, observations, instructions—on to some sort of permanent or semipermanent memory device. In most cases, that will be the hard drive of your computer. For the serious podcaster, it might be a separate digital recording unit. Or, if you're podcasting from the field (see Chapter 9, "Public Syndication"), it might be a small, portable recorder. In any case, this is the heart of the podcasting process.

"Groom" Your Podcast

When all of your content is recorded, no matter how brilliant it is, it's probably not quite ready for prime time yet. This part of the podcasting process is known as post-production and it's where you edit your podcast, enhance the audio quality of the basic recording, and preserve the final podcast in a digital format that's suitable for distribution. Some very successful podcasters devote as little time as possible to this part of the process, opting instead for what they believe is a more "authentic" sound. Other equally successful podcasters groom their podcasts carefully, often devoting three or four times as much time to post-production as they do to actual recording. As we'll see later, either approach can work, depending on the end result you want to achieve. Regardless of how much post-production is right for you, there's one indispensable aspect of post-production you can't neglect. Before you're done preparing your podcast, you've got to save it in a standard digital format that's accessible to as many potential listeners as possible. Almost always, this will mean saving your podcast as an MP3 file.

Post and Distribute Your Podcast on the Internet

Needless to say, the reason you're podcasting is to share your content with people who are interested in what you have to say. (Like the tree that falls in the forest, there's a philosophical question about whether or not it's really a podcast if no one can hear it!) The vehicle for reaching your listeners, of course, is the Internet. There are two elements involved in making your podcast available to the world. The first thing you'll need to do is to find a home on the Internet for the audio file that contains your podcast. The second requirement is to distribute it to interested listeners. The way to do this is to provide them with the means to subscribe to your podcast rather than having to manually search for it each time they want to listen. This subscription mechanism is known as an *RSS feed*, and you'll be learning all about it in Chapter 11, "Promoting Your Podcast." (*RSS* stands for *Really Simple Syndication*. Describing this technology as "really simple" proves that people in the computer industry have a sense of humor.)

It doesn't matter if you want to produce a podcast that's as polished as an NPR broadcast or something that feels raw, edgy, and spontaneous...or anything in between. Whatever "feel" you want to achieve, your podcast creation process will touch on each of these four basic steps.

MEET THE PODFATHER

Adam Curry is podcasting's most visible evangelist. His podcast, known as *The Daily Source Code*, is consistently among the industry's most popular podcasts. *The Daily Source Code* is eclectic, energetic, and unpredictable, featuring Adam's entertaining observations on podcasting, flying, music, or whatever else happens to be on his mind on a given day. A typical show will often feature Adam testing out a new piece of podcasting equipment and will include the results, whether they're good or bad. Adam sometimes provides his listeners with "soundseeing" tours of interesting locations when he's on the road. When he's at home, at "Curry Cottage" in Surrey, England, he will occasionally interview his lovely wife, Patricia Paay, creating what he refers to as a PPP (Patricia Paay Podcast). Adam's tireless efforts to promote podcasting have earned him a unique designation in the podcasting community: The Podfather!

Getting Inside the Listener Experience

Even though your focus in reading this book is on producing your own podcast, there are two important reasons why the best place to begin is to become familiar with what it's like to be a podcast consumer, or listener. The first is simply that listening to podcasts is very, very cool and we guarantee you'll enjoy it. The second, more important reason is that you cannot be a great podcaster—or, probably, even a very good one—if you aren't intimately familiar with every facet of your listeners' experience.

As radio guru Walter Sabo notes, each medium "has its own physics." To understand this better, consider the differences between movies and television. On the surface, they appear to be very similar—they both involve images that are viewed on a screen, for example—but that similarity only exists up to a point.

Movies are good at large, panoramic shots. Think of the battlefield scenes in *Star Wars*, for example. They lose their impact dramatically when they're taken off the large screen and scaled down for television. Television, on the other hand, can create a "cozy" environment with programs such as *Oprah* in a way that's impossible to achieve in a movie theater.

In much the same way, podcasts seem very similar to radio broadcasts. After all, they're both technologies that involve the dissemination of talk, music, and other audio content. A closer look at the way these two technologies work, however, reveals some important differences. If you're going to be successful as a podcaster, it's important that you understand these differences clearly.

Listening to podcasts is, unfortunately, a little more involved than just turning on the radio. That will certainly be changing rapidly as the software environment gets better and the infrastructure evolves. Right now, though, there are three steps your listeners need to take in order to listen to your podcasts. Your first important task as a budding podcaster, then, is to become a proficient podcast consumer by undertaking those same steps yourself. The three steps are discussed in the following sections.

Download and Install "Pod-catching" Software

It's certainly possible to scour the web for podcasts that might be interesting to you. Then, when you find one, you could go that podcast's website periodically to see if there's a new show. And, finally, when there is a new show, you could download it manually. All of that is possible, but it's quite labor intensive and very time consuming. If you had to go through that whole process every time you wanted to listen to a podcast, chances are you wouldn't end up doing very much listening.

The solution to this problem comes in the form of software that's specifically designed to help you find and download podcasts. Technically, the software packages that perform these functions are specialized RSS readers, but we're going to use the more popular designation and refer to them as "pod-catching" software. (Don't worry about the term *RSS* right now. We'll be exploring it in depth later on in the book.) By far, the most popular of these dedicated packages is called iPodder. (Of course, iTunes now has podcasting features, too. More about that in Appendix D.)

Point your browser to ipodder.org. From there, find the link that says Download iPodder. This link will take you to a screen (shown in Figure 1.1) that allows you to select the iPodder software designed for your computer's operating system.

Currently, you can download iPodder software for Windows, Macintosh, and Linux computers as well as Pocket PC devices and SmartPhones.

Just select the appropriate folder and download the software that's right for your computer. Once you've downloaded the software, follow the onscreen instructions to install it on your computer.

Your iPodder software performs all of the tasks associated with listening to podcasts that we identified a moment ago.

Find the Podcasts You Want and Subscribe to Them

iPodder software works with a podcast directory system that's maintained by volunteers. It's organized by category, as you can see in Figure 1.2. There are dozens of categories available and there are quite a few options in each category.

FIGURE 1.1
iPodder.org provides "pod-catching" software for a variety of operating systems.

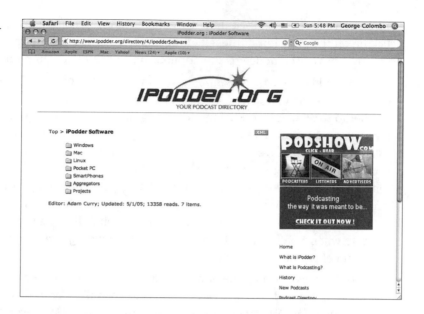

FIGURE 1.2
No matter what you're looking for, there's probably a category in the iPodder directory system that meets your needs perfectly.

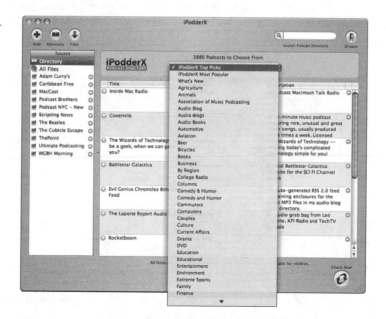

You can also get a directory listing, of the most popular podcasts or a listing of the podcasts that represent the top choices of the iPodder directory editors. While iPodder will allow you to add podcasts that you've found on the Web that aren't listed in its directory, chances are that the iPodder directory will provide all of the podcast browsing options you want.

Once you've found a podcast that looks interesting, you can then subscribe to it by clicking on the plus sign at the left of the podcast's listing. In Figure 1.1, the podcasts that have been added as subscriptions appear in the column on the left.

When you add a podcast subscription, you are given the option of downloading all available files, the first three files, or only the most recent file. You can also choose whether to save the file in MP3 format or, if you're using iTunes to manage your music files, you can convert each podcast to Apple's AAC file format. (You can instruct iPodder to move your files directly into iTunes if you want, or you can instruct the software to save them at a specified location on your hard drive.) Converting your downloaded podcasts to AAC creates a larger file. An important benefit of the AAC format, however, is that your podcast becomes "bookmarkable," so that if you leave your podcast before you're through listening to it, you can return to where you stopped listening rather than starting over again from the beginning of the file.

Once you've subscribed to one or more podcasts, you have a couple of options for downloading the podcast files. One option is to open iPodder and download any available new podcasts by clicking the Check Now button. The second option, however, is the one that most people select. In the software's Preferences settings, you can tell iPodder to check for and download new shows automatically, as shown in Figure 1.3.

FIGURE 1.3

Selecting Auto Check tells iPodder to automatically find and download new shows for the podcasts you've subscribed to.

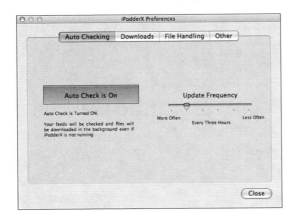

When you tell iPodder to Auto Check, the podcasts you want will automatically be downloaded to your computer. Once the podcasts you want to hear are on your hard drive, they can also be automatically synchronized with your portable music device. This can be your portable music player (an iPod, for example), a Pocket PC or other PDA-type device, or a Smart Phone.

Listen to Your Podcasts in "The Real World"

Of course, listening to the podcasts you've subscribed to would seem to go without saying. The important part of this step for you as a podcaster, though, is the part about listening in "the real world." An enormous mistake that many potential podcasters make is to only listen to podcasts in an office or studio environment. You'll be better prepared to create terrific podcasts if you spend some time listening to podcasts in listening environments that are like the ones from which your audience is likely to listen.

Listen to your favorite podcasts in your car on the way to work or while you're out doing errands. Listen to them while you're exercising. (If you don't already exercise regularly, here's another good reason to get started!) Listen to them while you're out shopping or in line at the post office. (You can save the longer podcasts for when you're waiting in line at the post office. They'll come in handy.)

Listening to podcasts out in "the real world" will teach you some lessons that will come in handy when you begin creating your own podcasts. You'll get a feel for how background noise in the listening environment changes the listening experience. You'll also have a chance to start to start thinking about what it takes to hold your listeners' attention. Did you find your attention drifting as you listened to a particular podcast? If you did, what was happening on the show—or not happening on the show—when it lost you?

Following these three steps will be entertaining but it will also be enlightening. It will turn you into a connoisseur of podcasts and a real student of the medium. You should think of this process as Podcasting 101. It will provide a foundation for your podcasting success.

The Differences Between Radio and Podcasting

Now that you're a seasoned podcast consumer, some of the dissimilarities between listening to podcasts and listening to radio are no doubt coming into focus for you. Let's take a moment before we go on to explore some of the more important differences.

Podcasting Time-shifts the Radio Experience

The most significant difference between podcasting and radio is that radio is a "real-time" audio medium, while podcasting time-shifts audio content for your listeners.

Time-shifting means that listeners have control over how and when they listen. Podcasting time-shifts audio content in the same way that TiVo time-shifts television content. Time-shifting allows a listener to check out your podcast whenever he or she wants. It also allows listeners to pause, rewind, and/or fast-forward.

To appreciate this difference, think about listening to the radio in your car on the way to work. It's 8:55 and you're running late for an important 9:00 a.m. meeting. As you pull into the parking lot, your favorite talk show host introduces a special guest. Maybe it's someone who's been in the news lately or an actress you've been a fan of for years. You really want to hear what the guest has to say...but you can't be late for your meeting. You turn off your car's ignition with a sigh of disappointment, knowing that you'll never hear the interview.

Time-shifting changes all that. It gives the listener complete control over when and how often the content is heard.

To say that content is time-shifted is not quite the same as saying that it's recorded. In today's high-tech radio environment, a great deal of what you hear is recorded rather than live, probably much more than you realize. But when radio content is recorded, a listener still has to listen to it at the precise time it's being broadcast. Otherwise it's gone forever.

So, what difference does time-shifting make? For your listener, it's extremely convenient, even empowering. But for you as a podcaster, it means you don't have any control over when your show is heard. That means you can't fill your show with some of the traditional staples of broadcast radio such as weather, traffic, and time-checks. It also means that if you're discussing or referencing something that's timely, you'll need to find a way to put your discussion into a time context for your listeners.

Finally, time-shifting means that if and when you want to generate revenue with your podcasts, you'll probably need to do so in a way that acknowledges your listener's ability to fast-forward past conventional 30-second commercials. Your business model will need to be more creative than the straightforward selling and placement of advertising that radio stations can use.

In short, time-shifting is a subtle but profound difference that significantly distinguishes podcasts from radio broadcasts.

Your Podcast Isn't Restricted by Programming Constraints

A radio show occupies a particular slice of time that's assigned to it by the programmer at the radio station. No matter what, it has to fill up that slice of time. A talk show host may run out of things to say on a particular subject but that doesn't relieve him or her of the need to keep on talking (or doing something!) until the end of the show's time slot.

Podcasts, on the other hand, don't operate under the same set of requirements. As a podcaster, your show can be structured to reflect the demands of your content, not the demands of the clock on a studio wall. If you've covered everything that needs to be covered then you're done. If there's a great deal that needs to be said about a particular subject, then there's no need to conclude your discussion at any particular time. Podcasting allows you to concentrate on content rather than format.

Podcasts Persist

The moment something gets played or said on the radio, it's gone forever. The brilliant quip or entertaining story you heard on the way to work is gone. You can't listen to it again and you can't share what you heard. Yesterday's radio show only exists in your memory.

Yesterday's podcast, on the other hand, remains on the Web for a while and then might remain on your mp3 player indefinitely. This has certain legal ramifications regarding what you can do on a podcast with someone else's music (much more on that later), but it also affects decisions you might make about the content you're going to create.

In this regard, the difference between a radio show and a podcast is like the difference between a remark that you might make to some co-workers in the hall at work and what you would choose to put in a memo. You're going to be a little more careful about the latter than you will the former.

The fortunate corollary to this principle is that you always have the opportunity to edit your podcasts before they're distributed. Even if your podcast is designed to sound completely spontaneous, the time gap between recording and distributing is a kind of safety net that you might choose to employ from time to time when you consider the fact that your podcast can remain on someone's computer or mp3 player forever.

THE ABSOLUTE MINIMUM

- Podcasting may seem similar to traditional radio broadcasting but it is a new and different medium all its own.

- Podcasts come in all sorts of different formats. Some of these trace back to traditional radio formats but many are unique to this medium.

- There are four basic steps to podcasting: Planning your podcast, recording your podcast, "grooming" your podcast, and posting and syndicating it.

- The first step to becoming a great podcaster is to become a voracious consumer of podcasts.

PART

CREATING A COMPELLING PODCAST

2

GUIDELINES FOR DESIGNING A KILLER PODCAST

Every great podcast begins with a vision. That's true if you want to create a straight-laced podcast for a niche in the tech community or a cutting-edge podcast featuring the latest indie rock.

Over the next few chapters, you'll learn how to turn your broad ideas into a fully conceptualized show. In this chapter, we'll start with the top level planning you'll need to undertake if you want to create a killer 'cast!

Begin with Your Listeners in Mind

Chances are, you have a broad idea in mind about what you want to do with your podcast. Your idea might still only be very general. Or podcasting might be something you've been considering for a while and, as a result, you have some very specific ideas in mind about what you'd like to do with your show.

If you're only interested in doing the show you've envisioned and you don't particularly care if anyone wants to listen to it or not, then you can disregard at least some of the advice in this chapter. (That's not necessarily a bad thing, by the way. After all, it's *your* podcast!) On the other hand, if you'd like to create a podcast that's widely subscribed to by an enthusiastic audience, the first thing you should do is forget about your concept for your show—at least for the time being. Instead of beginning your planning with the show concept, start by thinking about your prospective listeners. Ask yourself this question:

If my podcast becomes wildly successful, who will likely be listening to it?

If broadcasting is…well, broad, then podcasting is specific. The most effective podcasts in any genre aren't for everyone and don't try to be. Instead, each one appeals to a very specific group of listeners. (Two of the most popular podcasts at *Podcast Alley* are *The Dawn and Drew Show* and *The Catholic Insider*. Believe us, those two podcasts have very different, very specific audiences.)

Let's begin a brief exercise that will help you to better understand the most important component of your podcast: Your listener.

The First Step in Defining Your Listener

Who will want to listen to your podcast? Of course, no audience will ever be completely homogenous, but many of your potential listeners will likely have some similarities. Think about what your listeners will look like in terms of these characteristics:

- Age
- Gender
- Educational background
- Socio-economic background
- Entertainment interests
- Family and relationship interests
- Political leanings
- Interest in social issues or causes
- Hobby interests
- News interests
- Literary and artistic interests
- Occupational interests
- Business and financial interests
- Technology interests
- Religious affiliation
- Lifestyle interests

Your podcast will appeal to its listeners in a way that relates to one or more of these characteristics. Your listeners might share an interest in a particular hobby such as chess, for example. In that case, they might all be somewhat varied when it comes to the other characteristics. Or they might share two or more characteristics. An example of that might be Beatles fans under 20.

Drilling Down Another Level

Now that you've started to form a picture of who your listener is, let's take our exercise down to another level of specificity.

What do you know about how your listeners will likely want to consume your podcast? Most of the time, are they likely to

- Listen on a disk-based or a flash-based MP3 player?
- Listen on their computers?
- Listen while they're driving?
- Listen while they're working?
- Listen while they're exercising?
- Listen sporadically or regularly?
- Listen all week or only on business days?
- Download your shows manually or with pod-catching software?

Can you see how the answers to these questions can impact the choices you'll make as you design your show? (Stay with us. We'll have some very specific examples in a second.)

Of course, right now you're mostly just taking educated guesses about all of this. That's fine. Later on in the process, as you begin to actually develop an audience, we'll start adjusting your listener profile based on actual information.

Designing a Show That's Right for Your Listeners

The mental picture of your listeners that you're developing will affect decisions you make about your podcast throughout the rest of your planning process—and beyond. The clearer this picture is, the easier it will be for you to make decisions about format, length, frequency, and a variety of other attributes of your show.

Crafting the Best Overall Sound for Your Podcast

The best way to begin designing your show is to think a bit about what you want for your show's overall sound and feel. For example, Adam Curry's Daily Source Code has a distinctive sound and structure, one that's very different from The Dawn and Drew Show or Dave Winer's Morning Coffee Notes. What kind of overall structure makes sense for your show and what are your options? Well, here are some questions you might want to ask yourself for starters:

- Should my show be a soliloquy or do I want to break it up with music, interviews, or sound effects? (More on all of those in the next chapter, by the way.)
- Should it be ad-libbed or scripted?
- Is a slow, deliberate pace appropriate for your audience or would your show sound better at a breakneck, MTV-style pace?
- Do I want the audio quality to be pristine or should it have a funkier, more organic kind of sound?

If you're not sure what you want for your show's overall sound, think about two or three podcasts (or broadcast radio shows) that you enjoy and spend some time analyzing them with these questions in mind. Chances are, you've never had a reason to listen this analytically before. Breaking down the components of a favorite show's overall sound will likely give you some useful ideas about what you might want to do with your own show.

Choosing the Right Length

Do your listeners have the time or inclination to listen to a long show? Would they prefer to get information from you in relatively short, bite-sized chunks? Is file size/download time important to them? Your answers to all of these questions will help you determine an ideal target length for each show. Once you determine a target length, it's generally not a good idea to deviate from it significantly from one show to another.

For most listeners, 20 to 30 minutes is an ideal show length. For one thing, it means your podcasts won't produce inordinately large files. More important, though, is the fact that listeners tend to listen to podcasts in situations that overlay nicely with a 20 to 30 minute show, for example while exercising or while driving to work.

As a rule of thumb, you'll want to stick with your chosen target length as closely as you can for each show. If you need more time to cover a particular topic, it's generally better to break that topic up into multiple shows than it is to deviate from your target too much.

How Frequently Should You Post Your Shows?

One of the great things about podcasting as opposed to radio is that you don't have to accommodate a broadcast schedule. Since your show finds your listeners via RSS rather than forcing listeners to find your show, you can post shows with whatever kind of frequency you think would be best for your listeners. Do they want or need to hear from you on a regular basis? If you're dealing with subject matter that updates regularly, then a daily or weekly schedule might be appropriate. Alternatively, your listeners might prefer to hear from you only when there's breaking news or something important going on. For some listeners, a frequent podcast might be intrusive.

Here are some guidelines you can start with based on the listener characteristics you've already started considering:

Table 2.1 Podcast Design Guidelines

If Your Listeners Are	Then Your Podcast Should Probably Be
Listening while they're driving to work or exercising	Between 20 and 30 minutes long
Looking for hard, practical information	Well organized and deliberately paced
Listening for entertainment	More energetic and upbeat
Traditional and conservative	Created with an eye toward audio quality and production values
Students	Faster paced with a lot of variety
High tech	Higher quality, larger files
Low tech	Lower quality, smaller files
Checking and downloading your shows manually or listening to them in a browser	Posted on a regular schedule
Using pod-catching software	Posted when the content and show format dictates
Businesspeople	Concise and explanatory

This list is by no means comprehensive. Use it as a starting point to put together your own list. The idea here is for you to start looking at the design of your podcast critically from the very beginning and to get in the habit of making design decisions based on the likely desires of your listeners rather than just your own preferences.

Practice, Test, Practice Some More

In a little while, you'll be recording your first test podcasts. When you do, here is a critically important truth that is easy—and dangerous—to overlook:

It is impossible to be 100 percent right when you guess about what your audience likes and wants.

The whole process of designing your podcast and getting it right is an iterative one—in other words, an ongoing process of making decisions, getting feedback, making adjustments, and then getting more feedback.

Therefore, when you record your first several podcasts, think of them as "practice 'casts." If you're like almost every other budding podcaster, you'll think your practice 'casts suck. That's fine. You're supposed to think that. (Why should it be easier for you than it was for everyone else?)

But however much they might suck, the important thing is that they're a starting point and they're the foundation for you to get better and better as you continue to practice.

If you listen to these practice 'casts critically and make adjustments based on what you hear, you might fix a few obvious flaws but you haven't really made any progress with the iterative process we discussed a moment ago. In order to make progress, you need feedback.

Getting Feedback on Your Practice 'Casts

The best place to start getting feedback is with family and friends. Everyone's feedback can be helpful, of course, but the most important feedback you'll get at this stage will come from people you know who are as similar as possible to the listener profile you started developing earlier in this chapter. If you're launching a podcast for goth teens, for example, it's unlikely that the feedback you get from Uncle Marvin in Peoria will be as useful as what you get from your 18-year-old cousin Seth who had his tongue and eyebrow pierced and wears mascara.

Find four or five people in your Address Book who are close to the listener profile you have in mind and who wouldn't mind listening to your practice 'casts. You can think of this assemblage as your own private focus group. Now, send them your podcasts as they're created and ask for their honest opinions. When you do so, make it clear that you aren't fishing for compliments, that you really want their honest feedback on what would make your podcast better for them as a listener.

Some logistical considerations: If you have a website already, you can upload your podcast to your website and then just send a link to the people in your focus group. If you don't have a website, you'll probably want to send them the MP3 file of your podcast.

Since podcast files can be fairly large—often 15 or 20 megabytes or more—you might encounter problems sending the files via email since many email servers limit the files size they'll accept. An elegant solution to this problem can be found at this website: www.yousendit.com.

This site allows you to email a file that's up to 1 gigabyte in size. Using just your browser, you can send files as easily as simply filling out a short form as shown in Figure 2.1.

Until you have created a home on the Web for your podcasts, this is the easiest way for you to send podcasts—or any other types of files—that are larger than a megabyte or so.

FIGURE 2.1

Using yousendit.com, you can send files that are considerably larger than your regular email system might allow.

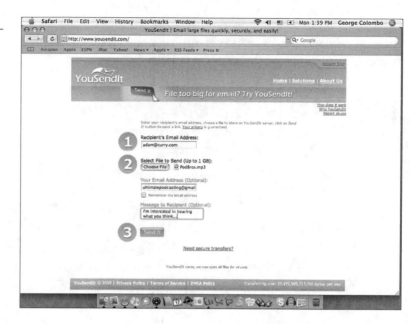

When you've gotten feedback from your first practice 'cast, make one or two changes based on what you've learned, then start the process all over again with another test podcast.

Don't expect one or two practice 'casts to be enough to get everything right. You should plan on five or six practice 'casts...and even more than that is perfectly reasonable. What's the right number of practice 'casts? As many as it takes for you to begin to feel comfortable and to feel as though your podcast is connecting with the members of your focus group.

DESIGN YOUR SHOW LIKE THE PROS

You see ads on TV for a brand new talk show and you decide to tune in to the show's premier. Since this is the very first episode of the show, you'll be able to see its development from the very beginning, right?

Actually, by the time a new talk show makes it onto some network's schedule, the producers have already shot several test shows. After every show, the production company gets detailed feedback from audience members and makes adjustments in the show. Sometimes, those adjustments consist of fine-tuning the host's delivery or some other element of the production. Sometimes, however, shows undergo major overhauls based on what the producers learn during this process.

In any event, the show's premier episode you get to watch is really the end result of an extensive practice and testing process that the general public never gets to see (except, perhaps, in a "bloopers" show 10 years later).

So, how does something like *The Dennis Miller Show* ever get on the air? Well, that's a great question but the answer is beyond the scope of this book!

Now that you understand the process of designing your podcast, let's turn our attention in the next chapter to the various component parts that will make up your podcast and see how each one of them is used.

THE ABSOLUTE MINIMUM

As you begin to design your podcast, you'll want to follow a process that will help your design meet the needs of your listeners.

- The best way to begin designing your podcast is to create a mental picture of your listeners.

- Consider standard demographic characteristics as well as any characteristics that are likely to derive from the theme and focus of your podcast.

- You should make decisions about the elements of your podcast based on who your likely listeners are and how they will likely be listening.

- Fine-tune your show design based on feedback you get from family and friends who are similar to your target audience.

- It will probably take several practice podcasts—and the feedback you get from each one—before your show concept starts to really come together.

3

THE COMPONENTS OF YOUR PODCAST

When you listen to a great podcast, it feels like magic. A great podcast grabs the listener by the collar and doesn't let go until it's finished. The challenge of creating that kind of magic might seem daunting but it's a lot like the old joke about eating an elephant: It's a lot easier if you approach it one bite at a time.

Some of the elements described in this chapter will appear in every show you create. You'll use others seldom, if at all. That's okay but it's still worthwhile to understand all of them. Think of these elements as tools in your podcasting toolkit. There are plenty of tools you don't use every day but, when that special occasion arises, there's nothing like having exactly the right tool.

In this chapter, we're going to break down the elements of your podcast and you're going to learn how to use each of the tools at your disposal as effectively as possible.

The Voice(s) on Your Podcast

Podcasting is an audio medium that's extremely personal. Unlike radio, which is often listened to in a car or in an office or in some other semi-public setting, podcasts are almost always listened to by one person at a time. As a result, you're communicating with your listener on a one-to-one basis.

But it goes even beyond that. Often, your listener is listening to you on a portable music player. When you think about it, then, you're talking right into your listener's ear. That's a very personal way to communicate. (Think about it! How often—and under what circumstances—do people talk directly into your ear? It's a very, very personal method of communication.)

It stands to reason, then, that the single most important factor in your podcast's success is going to be the connection that your listener feels with the voice he is hearing through his earbuds. For the most part, that voice is going to be you. In addition to your own voice, you may choose to add one or more other voices to your show.

In this discussion, when we talk about your voice, we're not using that word only in its traditional sense. We're not just talking about the quality of the sound that comes out of your mouth when you speak, but we're also talking about the personality that's projected by you and anyone else who's on your show regularly. We're also referring to the way all those personalities together contribute to the overall feel of the show.

Your Show Host Persona

There is no question about the fact that—regardless of the content or format of your show—the role you play as show host will be the single most important factor in determining whether or not your podcast is successful. There is no content that is so compelling or unique that it will make up for a show host who doesn't connect with the audience. On the other hand, there are podcasters who connect with their audiences so thoroughly that they're able to transcend occasionally mundane content and maintain an audience based on the sheer force of their personalities. This aspect of connecting with your audience begins with an understanding of something called *persona*. For the purpose of this discussion, we can define persona as *the personality or character that you consistently project to your audience.*

CLAP FOR THE WOLFMAN

One of the best known personas in the history of broadcasting belonged to a radio disk jockey named Bob Smith. If that name isn't familiar to you, you might recognize the name under which Bob worked in both radio and television for decades: Wolfman Jack.

Like all great broadcast personas, Wolfman Jack's persona was both carefully crafted and yet extremely natural. And, like all great personas, it was unique. When you heard the

Wolfman for the first time, his delivery cut through the airwaves like a beacon. It was unmistakable and differentiated him immediately from every other voice on the radio.

The Wolfman might not be a model for your persona, but you can learn a great deal about crafting a persona by studying what Bob Smith accomplished. You can learn more about this late, great, Hall of Fame personality by going to www.wolfmanjack.org or by renting a copy of *American Graffiti* the next time you're at the video store.

Persona is far more than just your voice or what you say on your podcast, although both of those things contribute to it. Persona is the aggregate of several factors, including your

- Voice
- Attitude
- Delivery
- Sense of humor
- Political perspective
- Social perspective
- Sense of playfulness
- Sense of outrageousness
- Energy level
- Vocabulary

There are no set rules for formulating a winning persona for your podcast. To a large extent, your persona is something that will develop over time as you become comfortable with the podcasting medium.

At this point in the discussion—especially if you have not had the opportunity to spend much time behind a microphone—there's a question that may be floating around in your mind somewhere. If you're like many people who hear about this concept for the first time, you may be thinking to yourself, "I don't want to develop some sort of phony persona. I just want to be myself on my podcast. What should I do in that case?"

This question is certainly not uncommon. It arises from an understandable tendency to confuse the concepts of playing a role and projecting a persona.

When you play a role, you're adopting a character and personality that is not yours. It's similar in many ways to improvisational acting. Adopting a character is one way to create a persona, to be sure, but it's certainly not the only way nor is it necessarily the best way.

Projecting a persona, on the other hand, is not in any way inconsistent with being yourself. It does mean that if you're going to be yourself, you need to do so in a way that (1) is consistent over time so that members of your audience get what they expect and (2) clearly projects to your audience through your medium.

Being consistent doesn't mean that your tone doesn't vary from one show to the next. In fact, it can—and probably should—vary considerably. One day you might be angry; another day you might be ecstatic. Those kinds of variations can be distinctly positive. (Keep that in mind as we discuss predictable unpredictability in a bit.) Consistency means that your audience can hear your underlying persona no matter what kind of mood you're in.

The ability to project is the other significant factor in crafting your persona. Think of your podcast persona as a music player. If you were to adopt a character as part of your persona, that would be like changing the song that's playing. Projecting your persona, by contrast, is more like just turning up the volume a little bit. Your listeners won't engage with a persona that doesn't project any more than the people they're already talking to every day.

TURNING UP THE DIAL

Projecting your persona might not be something you've thought about before, but the results that come out of a set of speakers or a pair of earbuds are unmistakable.

Try this experiment: Sit down with a friend and some recording equipment. Record the results as you speak in a normal, conversational tone. Take no more than two minutes to tell your friend what your favorite CD is and give two or three reasons why you like it.

Now, get ready to re-record yourself taking the same two minutes and making the same two or three points. This time, however, create a mental image for yourself of an imaginary dial that controls how much you project as you speak. Turn the dial up about 20 percent, then make your recording. Listen to the two recordings, one after the other, and the difference will be clear.

If it's going to be successful, your podcast needs to be engaging and entertaining. (There's a reason we refer to each episode as a "show"!) All of that begins with your persona. What you now know that many podcasters don't is that your persona doesn't develop by accident.

Do You Need (or Want) a Co-Host?

Your decision about whether or not to have a co-host for your podcast is entirely subjective; ultimately, there's no answer that's definitively right or wrong.

There are a number of plausible reasons for going it alone:

- You may value the flexibility of not having to coordinate with another person to create a show
- Your vision for your podcast may be a very personal one that would not easily accommodate another personality

- Your podcast is specifically designed to promote you as a personality or some product or service you're involved with
- Your kindergarten report card said, "Does not play well with others"

On the other hand, there are some great reasons to have a co-host:

- Your podcast was conceived as a joint venture with someone you like or someone with whom you share a business interest
- You want to balance a couple of different perspectives
- You know someone who can bring some quality or expertise to your podcast that you can't provide by yourself
- You want to share the workload of regularly producing a podcast with someone else

If you decide to have a co-host for your podcast, there are a few rules you'll want to keep in mind to make the arrangement work as well as possible for you, your co-host, and—most importantly—for your listeners.

If Possible, Have Distinctly Different Voices

Ever wonder why so many radio teams are comprised of one male and one female? This isn't the only reason or even the most important one, but it certainly is a significant factor. Keep in mind the fact that your listener—unlike a television viewer—has no visual cues to differentiate one voice from the other.

One very popular podcast is hosted by two brothers who sound a great deal alike. Of course, there's not a great deal that can be done about it. After all, brothers do tend to sound alike. Still, the situation can be confusing to the show's listeners, especially newer ones who have not learned over time to distinguish one brother from the other.

Like the situation with these two brothers, you many not have a great deal of control over this aspect of your show. If you do have control over it, though, and if you have a choice, pick a co-host who has a voice that is distinctly unlike yours.

WHAT TO DO WHEN TWO VOICES SOUND ALIKE

Unless you or your co-host is willing to try to adopt a completely different "on-air" voice (not recommended), your best bet it to get in the habit of giving your listener cues to differentiate between two similar voices.

The easiest and most effective cue is to use each other's names as often as possible. (In fact, whether your voices are similar or not, this is still a pretty good practice.) Of course, there's a point at which that becomes distracting. Precisely where that point lies is a judgment call that you'll have to make. In any event, you'll be doing your listener a favor if you use names noticeably more often than you'd use them when you're not podcasting.

Don't Talk Over Each Other

This is a variation of the same issue you face when you're dealing with two similar voices: Your podcast cannot provide your listener with visual cues about what's going on. What might come across on television as an energetic exchange of views will simply sound garbled on your podcast.

There's nothing wrong with an energetic exchange of views. The trick to making that work on your podcast is to simply take turns. It's not something that necessarily comes naturally—and it's easy to forget in the heat of the moment—but with a little bit of practice, you can establish the habit of not stepping on each other's lines.

Assume Distinct Roles in the Podcast

There's an old adage that says if two people agree about everything, then one of them is unnecessary. That's not a bad rule to follow on your podcasts. In addition, there's a corollary you can add to the rule: If two co-hosts are performing the same functions on the show, one of them is superfluous.

The most engaging co-host pairings generally work in one of two different ways:

- The two hosts are adversarial and disagree about almost everything. The Fox News pairing of Hannity and Colmes is a perfect example of how this type of co-hosting arrangement works.

- One co-host is somewhat subservient to the other. This co-host functions not quite as an equal but, instead, acts as a surrogate voice for the listener. He or she asks the questions a listener might ask and reacts out loud in ways that a listener might. Think of Robin Quivers and Howard Stern.

Creating distinct roles for each of your podcast's co-hosts has one additional benefit. No matter how charismatic you are, chances are you'll rub some listeners the wrong way. If your co-host's role is differentiated from yours in a meaningful way, you increase the likelihood that any given listener will be able to find someone on the show with whom he or she can establish a bond.

Conducting Interesting Interviews

Interviews are a staple of the podcasting world—and with good reason. An interview is a terrific way to bring to your audience content that goes beyond what you're able to provide yourself. Handled properly, it is also an engaging device. Good interviews sound spontaneous, conversational, and thoughtful—all appealing qualities for your listeners.

The most important factor in crafting an interview that your audience will find interesting is to find interesting guests. What makes a guest interesting in an interview is not how much he or she knows but rather how well he or she can communicate. Every veteran interviewer has multiple war stories about guests who looked qualified on paper but were a bust when they got in front of a microphone.

A helpful approach for avoiding that kind of uncomfortable situation is to schedule your interviews, whenever possible, on the phone rather than via email. This technique will give you a general (if not necessarily perfect) sense of your subject's style and level of communications skills. It can't guarantee you a terrific interview each time but every once in a while it can help you avoid a complete stinker!

In Chapter 7, "Recording Your Podcast," we'll be exploring some much more specific tips and techniques for conducting effective interviews. For our purposes right now, however, it's enough to note that a well executed interview can be an important and useful device in your podcasting toolkit.

Using Music Skillfully

As an aspiring podcaster, you might be wondering, "Is it really necessary for me to learn how to use music?" Our answer to this question is, "Only if you want people to listen!" In fact, music accomplishes a number of important objectives that would be very difficult, if not impossible, to accomplish in any other way.

Of course, if you're producing a music-centric podcast, the value of the music is self-evident. Don't, however, overlook the importance of music in your talk format show. Skillfully deployed in your podcast, music can

- Grab your listener's attention
- Establish a mood for your podcast
- Add humor to your podcast
- Enhance your podcast's overall listenability
- Makes your podcast sound more professional and polished

Occasionally, a highly targeted niche podcast will persist without music in much the same way that a quantum mechanics professor gets away with wearing two different socks—the content of what's being delivered is so specialized and so targeted that normal rules become less relevant. Even in such cases (which, by the way, will not apply to the overwhelming majority of podcasters), a little bit of attention to aesthetic elements like music will pay large dividends in overall quality that listeners perceive.

One important caveat: There are serious intellectual property implications surrounding your ability to use music in your podcasts. We'll be discussing these in greater

tip

The term for the music that's played at the beginning and end of your show is "bumper music" or simply "bumpers."

detail later on. In the meantime, though, if you want quality bumper music you can use without worrying about licensing implications, here are a couple of sites that might have what you're looking for:

http://www.shockwave-sound.com/

http://www.stockmusic.net/

Figure 3.1 shows the kind of options that will be available to you when you browse through these sites or others like them. (Google the term "stock music" and you'll find more.)

FIGURE 3.1

You can find music for your podcast on a stock music site such as shockwave-sound. com.

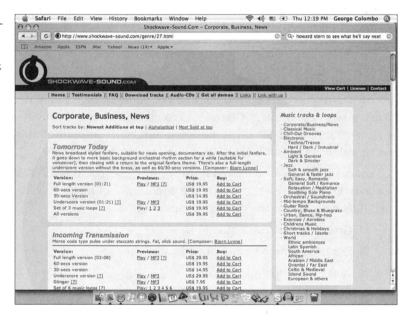

Both sites have high-quality content and both allow you to pay a nominal fee for virtually unlimited use. Most of the time, you'll have the option of downloading an entire song or just downloading a 30- or 60- second clip if that's all you'll need (at a significant savings, of course). Best of all, both sites allow you to preview as many songs as you want, as often as you want, guaranteeing that the music you download will be precisely what you want.

Sound Effects

You've heard these all your life on the radio and on television. They've been a staple of broadcasting for generations. When someone makes a funny mistake on the air, for example, it can be even funnier if it's immediately followed by a judiciously placed "Boing!" sound. Other common sound effects include

- Laughing
- Phones ringing
- Traffic noise
- Various bodily functions (use your imagination)
- Explosions or gunfire
- Crowd noises
- Applause

Most of the time, these kinds of sound effects are used for humorous purposes. Occasionally, though, they can be used to enhance a serious narrative or to emphasize a point.

In the early days of podcasting (back in late 2004!), adding sound effects was a laborious process. Unlike DJs on the radio who had machines specifically designed for sound effects, there was simply no convenient way for most podcasters to add sound effects into a show as it was being recorded. As a result, they usually opted to not use them rather than investing the time it took to add them to a show in post-production.

Today's podcasting software makes it much easier to work with sound effects and to add them into your podcast on the fly.

Sound effects are available from a variety of sources. Some podcasters record their own. There are also websites that offer bundles of sound effects you can purchase online or on CD. This website is a good place to start: `http://www.a1freesoundeffects.com/radio.html`.

You'll find dozens of sound effects that are available to you free for non-commercial use.

Balancing Quality and "Realism"

Some podcasts are the result of a great deal of time and effort spent in post-production. Others are clearly the result of someone hitting the "Record" button on their software, talking for some amount of time, hitting the "Stop" button, then posting the raw file on the Web.

Podcasters in the first category want to provide a flawless program with high-quality production values. *WGBH Morning Stories* is an example of this type of podcast. Listening to that particular podcast, it's reasonable to estimate that post-production takes four or five times as much time as the actual recording. The final product is pristine.

Adam Curry's *Daily Source Code*, on the other hand, is usually recorded in real-time and includes every hiccup and misstep he makes during the process. He'll experiment with new equipment and his listeners will hear the results—good, bad, or disastrous.

Which approach is correct? Well, both of those shows are among the most popular around so it's clear that there's an audience for either approach. What's important is that, once you've settled on a general approach, you remain relatively consistent. If you've opted to emphasize production values then your audience may find even a small glitch to be distracting. On the other hand, if your audience thinks it's getting a raw, unedited show and then hears an edit, you'll have a the beginnings of a credibility problem.

Unpredictability (Within a Framework)

Once someone has listened to your podcast two or three times, there are basically two reasons why he or she might stop. One reason is that she gets bored because she knows what to expect. The other reason is that she gets disoriented because she doesn't know what to expect. It's a tricky dynamic but your ability to master it can make your podcast downright compelling.

Your listeners will come to expect a predictable framework from your show. There are certain things they'll expect to hear each time they download a show and listen. If you fail to function within that framework, you'll create a disconnect with your audience.

At the same time, your listeners definitely won't continue to subscribe to your show if it gets too predictable. They want to be challenged and surprised. But here's the key principle to keep in mind: They can accommodate surprise much better if it's delivered within a predictable framework.

THE VALUE OF UNPREDICTABILITY

This scene from *Private Parts*, a movie about the career of the often outrageous radio personality Howard Stern, demonstrates the impact creative unpredictability can have on building your audience.

Researcher: The average radio listener listens for 18 minutes. The average Howard Stern fan listens for—are you ready for this?—an hour and twenty minutes.

Station Manager: How can that be?

Researcher: Answer most commonly given? I want to see what he'll say next.

Station Manager: Okay, fine. But what about the people who hate Stern?

Researcher: Good point. The average Stern hater listens for two and a half hours a day.

Station Manager: If they hate him, why do they listen?

Researcher: The most common answer? I want to see what he'll say next.

You might, for example, have an interview segment in every show. Within that segment, however, you might make it a practice to throw in outrageous questions. Or you might begin each show with a commentary segment that gets extreme or even shocking. Your listeners will appreciate both the outrageousness of your content and the predictability of your format.

Does that seem a bit inconsistent, even contradictory? Well, it probably is. That's why podcasting is as much of an art as it is a science. We're confident, though, that the tools you've discovered in this chapter will help you craft a podcast that grabs your listeners' attention and keeps them coming back for more.

THE ABSOLUTE MINIMUM

Building a great podcast is easier when you break it down into its component parts.

- Your show host persona will be the single most important element in creating a great show.

- While it's not necessary to work with a co-host, doing so can make your show sound better and make the job of producing it easier.

- Interviewing guests is a great way to deliver important information to your audience.

- Music and sound effects are valuable tools for crafting your podcast's overall sound.

- A creative balance between predictability and unpredictability will keep your listeners coming back.

4

STRATEGIES FOR PLANNING EACH SHOW

Podcasts come in all kinds of different formats and they appeal to all sorts of different audiences. In spite of all the differences, though, there's still one single factor that separates high-quality podcasts from second-tier efforts. That factor is preparation. In this chapter, you'll learn how to ensure a terrific podcast every single time you turn on your microphone.

The Basics of Show Preparation

Years ago, a friend of ours went to a Jethro Tull concert. (Our younger readers will have to take our word for the fact that Jethro Tull was a popular British rock band from the 1970s.) Our friend was impressed with everything about the show including the apparent abandon with which the members of the band jumped and ran around the stage as they played.

As it turned out, our friend was offered a ticket to see the band again the following evening, an offer he gladly accepted. As he began watching the band for the second night in a row, though, he realized something startling: Every movement had actually been planned. All the running, jumping, and gesturing that seemed so spontaneous the evening before was actually choreographed down to the smallest detail. The band members duplicated the previous evening's performance precisely.

There's an important lesson in this story, one that can elevate your podcast to a whole new level. Even if you want it to sound completely spontaneous, off-the-cuff, and unrehearsed, the most important factor in your podcast's success is still going to be how well you prepare for each show.

Show preparation consists of deciding what you're going to talk about on each show and planning the order in which the various topics and elements of your show are going to be discussed.

It would be almost impossible to overstate the importance of adequate show preparation. In fact, show prep is important for several reasons.

It Allows You to Approach Each Show More Confidently

Whether you're a veteran podcaster or you're getting ready to produce your first podcast, you still probably get a few butterflies in your stomach as you get ready to hit the "record" button on your software. This is a natural reaction that you probably won't ever lose completely.

You can, however, tame your butterflies considerably by being as prepared as you possibly can for each show. The time you invest in show prep will allow you to sit down in front of the microphone confident that the show you're about to create will be as entertaining and engaging as possible.

It Improves the Flow of Your Podcast

Consider this: Your audience is listening to your podcast on a computer or an MP3 player. In either case, there's a large number of entertainment alternatives available if your show starts to falter. That means you've got to hold your listener's attention from the beginning of your show to the end.

The most important factor in holding your listener's attention is the flow of your show. It has to move smoothly from start to finish and it's got to be engaging enough throughout to keep your listener from bailing out.

Adequate show prep will help you to manage the flow of your show and to make sure that there are no avoidable dead segments or awkward segues that might prompt your listener to turn her attention elsewhere.

It Guarantees You Won't Overlook Something You Wanted to Talk About

It's the end of your podcast. You wrap up by reminding your listeners of your email address and website. Then, just as you click the "stop" button to conclude your recording, you remember something you wanted to include in the show that slipped your mind while you were recording. At this point, you can either edit in the material you wanted to cover or you can wait until you record your next show.

Sure, this isn't exactly a tragedy…but it's certainly an annoyance. More importantly, it's an annoyance that could have easily been avoided with a bit more attention to show prep.

It Makes Post-Production Easier

One of the great things about podcasting is that it gives you the ability to clean up any rough edges before the show goes out to your listeners. Just because you're able to do that, though, doesn't mean that doing it is fun!

Your entire post-production process will be much easier and go much faster when you don't have to do a lot of editing. And you'll find that your need to edit will generally arise in inverse proportion to the quality of your show prep. This is significant when you consider that, for most podcasters, the majority of the time it takes to complete a podcast is taken up with post-production work.

Time-Tested Show Prep Techniques

Show preparation isn't difficult or mysterious. And, best of all, any time and effort you put into show prep will be paid back many times over in the quality of your podcasts and the ease with which you'll be able to produce them.

Some simple techniques—time-tested by podcasters and radio personalities alike—will allow you to approach your podcast with more confidence, cover all of the material you want to cover, and complete your post-production as painlessly as possible.

The ABC Technique (Always Be Clipping!)

Noted radio consultant Walter Sabo once observed that top-tier radio personalities spend four hours out of every day on the air and the remaining twenty hours engaged in show prep. His point was not that these broadcasters are constantly obsessing over their show. What Sabo meant was that top-tier broadcast personalities always keep their eyes and ears open for material that might be useful on the air. If you're going to be a top-tier podcaster, you'll want to do the same thing.

The technique is simple: Keep a file folder and a recorder handy. When you're thumbing through newspapers and magazines and you come across an item that you might want to use in your podcast, clip it out and drop it into your file folder.

The same principle applies to listening to the radio or watching television. Chances are, you own a portable recording device for recording sound-seeing tours or other podcasts from the field. (Because of their size and attractive pricing, Rio MP3 players with built-in recording technology tend to be most podcasters' portable recorder of choice.) When you hear something that might be useful or interesting, simply turn on your recorder and capture it.

Your objective is not necessarily to record the audio for use in your podcast (although that's certainly possible as long as you respect the appropriate copyright constraints). Instead, you simply want to capture the information or idea that struck you as interesting so that it's available when you sit down to plan your show.

The specific information you're looking for will depend, of course, on the nature of your show and your audience. If you're like most podcasters, your show probably targets a specific audience and you'll want to focus on those items that are most likely to interest them. Beyond that somewhat obvious strategy, you'll want to pay attention to your own instincts and reactions. If you find something interesting, chances are your audience will, too.

Collect More Than You Need (Way More!)

If you listen to talk radio, you'll hear a constant theme among the more popular hosts—and it doesn't matter whether they're conservative or liberal. Each host will phrase it differently, but every one expresses the same thought: "We've got so many things to talk about today, I don't know if we'll be able to get it all in."

You might to tempted to think that these hosts are simply hyping their shows to keep listeners tuned in…and there's certainly some of that going on. However, it's also true that these hosts are being accurate. They're not talking about the relative amount of news that's occurred on a given day, though. (After all, *every* day can't be a big news day!) What they're referring to is that fact that they are over-prepared. In the course of their show prep, they've collected more things to talk about than they'll ever have time to cover. It's an effective technique on the radio and it will work just as well for you in your podcast.

The Usual Suspects

Unless your podcast is highly specialized, you'll probably want to keep an eye on certain publications and websites that are reliable harbingers of trends in pop culture and/or technology. These resources, such as *The Drudge Report* shown in Figure 4.1, set the agenda for water cooler conversations across the country.

FIGURE 4.1

Love it or hate it, your listeners are probably looking at *The Drudge Report* regularly.

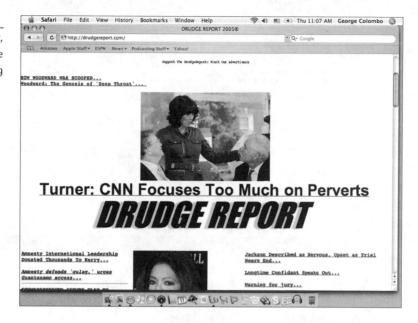

As you prepare for your podcasts, here are some of sites you should consider checking out:

- CNET News (http://news.com.com/)
- CNN (http://www.cnn.com/)
- *The Drudge Report* (http://drudgereport.com/)
- Google News (http://news.google.com/news)
- *The New York Times* (http://nytimes.com/)
- *USA Today* (http://usatoday.com/)
- Wired News (http://wired.com)
- Yahoo! News (http://news.yahoo.com/)

Almost all of these sites provide RSS feeds to which you can subscribe. This will make it easier for you to keep an eye on information and late-breaking news that might be of interest to you and your listeners. The summary of the *USA Today* RSS feed in Figure 4.2 shows how effective the technology can be at compiling and summarizing the news you need to know.

FIGURE 4.2

RSS provides convenient summaries of the news you need at a glance along with hyperlinks to more complete information.

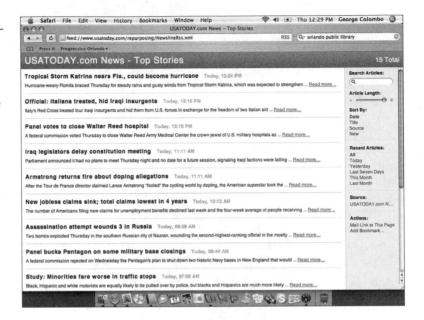

In addition to these sites for the general public, there are a few destinations on the Web that are specifically designed to assist with show prep for broadcasters and/or podcasters. A few of the more useful ones are

- Corey Deitz Show Prep Guide (http://www.radioearth.com/)
- Prep Links (http://www.preplinks.com/)
- Radio 411.com (http://radio411.com/prep.htm)

If you keep your show prep antennae tuned in to sources such as these—along with others you'll accumulate for yourself over time—you'll have gobs of material waiting whenever you decide to sit down and produce a show.

Design the Flow of Your Show

It's just about time to record another show. You've got a file folder full of interesting material you'll want to cover. What now?

Well, as we mentioned a moment ago, just having a file folder that's full of material will put you in a much better position than you'd be without it. But a just little more planning will yield even greater results from your show prep efforts.

MOLECULES OR ELECTRONS?

Much of your show prep work will be done online. As you find material on the Web, you're probably tempted to just save the bookmarks instead of printing out the material you discover. While it's certainly possible to do that, printing out your material and working from paper is a much better approach.

When you're recording your podcast, both you and your computer are going to be extremely busy. Moving back and forth between your web browser and your recording program introduces unnecessary opportunities for things to go awry. Working with print-outs of material you find on the Web will allow you to keep your computer focused on recording while you stay focused on the show.

Also, paper allows you to keep your material spread out in front of you. This is a much more functional approach than trying to navigate among multiple windows on your computer. Paper also allows you to easily highlight a particular item or passage so that you can refer to it quickly when you need it.

Finally, the rustling of paper as you move from one item to another can provide an audio flourish that enhances your show's listenability. (One prominent radio personality uses this trick as a staple in his nationally syndicated program.)

The following sections describe a three-step approach that will organize your show prep material for maximum usefulness.

Prioritize Your Material

Once you start recording a podcast, you'll often find that it takes on a life of its own. A show that you thought would take 15 or 20 minutes will sometimes whiz right past the half hour mark while you're feeling as though you're just warming up! (Conversely, of course, you'll occasionally find yourself covering one topic after another at a breakneck pace. That's why it's so important to be over-prepared!)

This part of your show prep begins, then, by performing a rough sort of the material you've collected into order of importance. The most important, must-discuss items should be placed into their own pile. Everything else goes into a second pile that consists of items that are interesting but not critical.

Mix Up Your Material by Topic

Your next step is to take a look at the items in your first pile and separate them by general topic. For example, let's say you're doing a podcast on science fiction. In your pile of show material, you find one article about an upcoming movie version of a Philip K. Dick novel. Somewhere else in the pile, there's an article that speculates on whether or not there's going to be a movie based on Marvel Comics's Dr. Strange. There are a couple of ways you might handle this.

One approach would be to group them together. If your treatment of each item is going to be brief, that could be a plausible option. A more likely scenario, though, is that you'll want to devote a bit of time to discussing each of those two similar items. In that case, it's much better to separate them in your podcast.

Look at it this way: Either your listener is interested in sci-fi movies or he's not. If he is interested, then he's much more likely to stick with your podcast after your discussion of the first movie so that he can hear you talk about the second one later on. If he's not interested in sci-fi movies, then he might stay with you for a discussion of one movie, but you'd certainly lose him if you talked about two in a row. In either instance, your prospects for keeping a listener's attention are improved when you separate similar topics.

Mix Up Your Material by Tone

Podcasting is, at its heart, entertainment. As a new medium, it is in the process of evolving some of its own rules. Even so, many of the basic rules that have developed over time in other media apply to you as a podcaster. One of these rules is that you should constantly vary the tone and pace of your show in order to keep your audience's attention.

On *The Tonight Show*, for example, you won't ever see two comedians on back-to-back. A singer in concert won't perform two ballads in a row. And *Good Morning America* will almost always alternate hard news segments with human interest segments. All of these entertainment outlets know that it's easy to lose an audience's attention with a monotonous format. They mix up the pace and tone of their shows—and you should, too.

If your podcast is about technology, for example, you might follow an analysis of Apple's new operating system with some listener feedback before you get into a review of the new line of iPods. Adam Curry's *Daily Source Code* provides a great example of this technique. There are several elements that are regularly featured in that podcast:

- Technical banter
- Non-technical banter
- Podsafe music
- Mashups
- Promos for other podcasts

Curry tries to mix these elements in a way that keeps his listeners' attention. That variety doesn't happen by accident. It's the result of a show prep process that follows the principles we've discussed here.

KEEP AN EYE ON THE CLOCK

As a podcaster, you don't have the same kinds of time constraints that radio personalities have. You don't have to break for news and traffic at the bottom of the hour and you don't have to end your show at a particular time.

Even so, it's a good idea to keep an eye on the clock as you record your show. For one thing, you'll probably want to keep each show within a certain time limit to keep the show's file size manageable. More important, though, is the fact that keeping an eye on the clock will help you manage your podcast's tempo. Your audience will appreciate the brisker pace that results. Just because you have all the time in the world doesn't mean you have to take it.

Don't Forget the Funny Stuff

If there's a podcast topic out there that wouldn't benefit from regular doses of levity, we have yet to find it.

Regardless of the topics you cover or the audience you're targeting, there's an important fact that many podcasters forget—and their shows suffer for it: Your audience wants to be entertained.

There is no information you can convey that's so unique that your audience can't find it somewhere else. And it's probably available somewhere in a format that's easier to get to than your podcast. Of course, you can add some value to the information as an aggregator, for example by collecting information from disparate sources and putting it together in a convenient format. Increasingly, though, technology continues to make it easier for your listener to perform that function without you.

The real value you add as a podcaster comes from your perspective and from the degree to which you're able to package content in a way your audience finds entertaining. There are a number of ways to be entertaining, of course, but none is as reliable as humor. This doesn't mean that your show needs to be funny all the time or that you need to be a comedian. It simply means that humor has proven to be a valuable tool for all sorts of broadcasters and it can work for you in your podcast, too.

You say you're not a natural humorist? That's why we're dealing with this subject in a chapter about show preparation. If you're no Rodney Dangerfield—and most of us aren't—you can still be funny enough to make a difference with a small amount of planning and preparation.

For starters, the same process that we discussed for general show prep also applies to using humor in your podcast. Keep your eyes and ears open for items that are amusing. When you come across something that makes you smile, giggle, or laugh out loud, make sure you clip it, record it, jot it down, or otherwise capture it. Beyond that, the show prep sites we've already mentioned all have links to humor pages and/or humor sites. These are the same resources that broadcast professionals use to interject humor into their shows.

BELIEVE IT OR NOT, YOU CAN LEARN TO BE FUNNY

Granted, if you're not comfortable with humor, it's unlikely that you'll turn into a great comic like Jerry Seinfeld or Lewis Black. Even so, humor is not an entirely innate skill. With a little bit of effort, you can learn to be funnier than you think you are today.

A great place to start is a book titled *Great Comedians Talk About Comedy* by Larry Wilde. (You can find it on Amazon or Barnes & Noble.) This crash course in the art of being funny features contributions from comedians such as Woody Allen, Milton Berle, Johnny Carson, and Jerry Seinfeld. If these guys can't show you how to be funnier then nobody can.

By the way, did you hear the one about the priest, the rabbi, and the podcaster…?

Avoiding the Cardinal Sin of Podcasting

Ultimately, there's only one sin from which your podcast can't recover:

- You can get away with being controversial
- You can get away with being opinionated
- You can get away with being outrageous
- You can get away with being arrogant and insufferable
- You can even get away with being wrong (which some podcasts are… regularly!)

The one thing you cannot afford to be is BORING!

Remember that your listener has literally thousands of podcasts from which to choose and he has a very limited attention span. As a result, you've got to hold his attention from the beginning of your podcast to the very end. That's the challenge you have as a podcaster.

The good news, though, is that as a podcaster you're not obligated to fill up a certain amount of air time gratuitously. Your show can be exactly as long as it needs to be to cover your material…and not a moment longer. That's a tremendous advantage. Combining that fact with the show prep techniques you learned in this chapter will ensure that your podcasts hold your listeners' attention and keep them coming back for more.

THE ABSOLUTE MINIMUM

- Show prep is the secret ingredient of successful podcasts.
- There are lots of resources at your disposal that can make show prep easy.
- The most effective podcasters keep their eyes and ears open constantly for material they can use in their podcasts.
- Humor is a tremendously effective tool for engaging listeners and it's not as difficult to use as you might think.
- The cardinal sin of podcasting is being boring.

5

CREATING A POSITIVE FEEDBACK LOOP WITH YOUR LISTENERS

The best podcasts are actually one end of an ongoing conversation that takes place between you and your listeners. Like most engaging conversations, your podcast will work best when you listen to the feedback you're getting and respond to it. In this chapter, you'll learn how to make your podcasts better by tapping into ideas and reactions from your audience.

Don't Podcast in a Vacuum

It's been said that on any given flight, an airplane is actually off course most of the time. Turbulence, wind gusts, and a number of other factors combine to keep pushing the airplane off its predetermined flight path. It's only through an ongoing series of mid-course corrections that the pilot is able to accurately guide the plane to its final destination. As you can imagine, though, the whole process would be a lot more difficult without constant feedback from observations and instruments. In fact, without that feedback, it would be virtually impossible to get where you want to go.

The same idea holds true for your podcast: It will be just about impossible for you to consistently create great podcasts without regular feedback from your listeners.

This principle isn't unique to podcasting. In fact, every communications and entertainment medium deliberately solicits input from its readers, listeners, or viewers:

- Many media outlets use focus groups and surveys to find out what their audiences think about their content.
- Most radio stations carefully monitor their phone calls for listener feedback.
- Radio and television stations often use surveys to find out what's working and what's not.
- Ratings services provide broadcast media with detailed information about what audiences want.
- Every media organization monitors its mail—electronic and traditional—to see what's hot and what's not.

Keeping your finger on the pulse of what listeners are thinking is every bit as important to your podcast as it is to large media companies. The bad news is that it's unlikely you have the same kind of budget available to support those types of efforts. The good news, though, is that you don't need a big budget to stay close to your audience. There are several low-cost and no-cost options available to you. Some combination of them will be just what you need in order to make sure your podcast is responsive to your listener community.

Your Show Notes/Blog

The overwhelming majority of podcasts use blogging software as the foundation of their website. This isn't just an arbitrary convention that developed over time. There are several good reasons to structure your website as a blog.

For one thing, blogging software makes it easy to update the content of your website. When you post a new podcast and you want to add show notes, blogging is the simplest, most straightforward way to do so.

Another reason to use blogging software is that it allows you to add show notes or other content from any computer that's connected to the Internet. It doesn't matter where you are. As long as you have access to a browser, you're in business.

The final reason to use blogging software is that it provides a quick and convenient way for your listeners to provide you with feedback.

When you post show notes in a blog format, you can include a link at the end of each post that allows users to make a comment. For example, Figure 5.1 shows the show notes for Garrick Van Buren's *First Crack* podcast with links after each post to comments from listeners.

FIGURE 5.1

First Crack show #43 received one comment from a listener while show #42 received two comments.

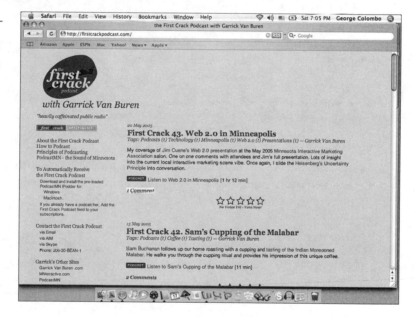

When a listener clicks on the comment link, he or she is immediately presented with a form that allows them to post comments, as shown in Figure 5.2.

Of course, it would be just as simple to create a link that would allow your listener to send you an email. Why not do that instead of having them leave a post on your website? Well, actually you should do *both*, as we'll see in a moment. However, there are some important advantages that posted listener feedback has over email.

■ Using a form to post feedback is faster and easier for your listener.

■ Posted comments permit the option of anonymous feedback. Of course, you have the option of not allowing anonymous posting (and there are certainly valid reasons for exercising that option). If you choose to allow this practice, though, a feedback form is the easiest way to do it.

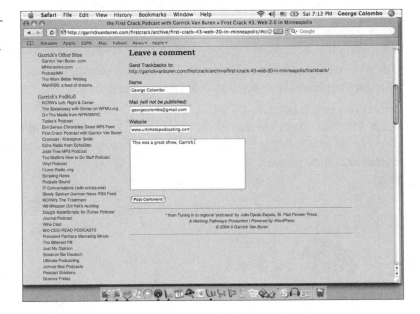

- When posted comments are used on your website, listeners can see each others' comments. This encourages further postings. In effect, the thread of postings can evolve into a "conversation." Figure 5.3 shows part of a thread of postings from the website of *The Dawn and Drew Show*.

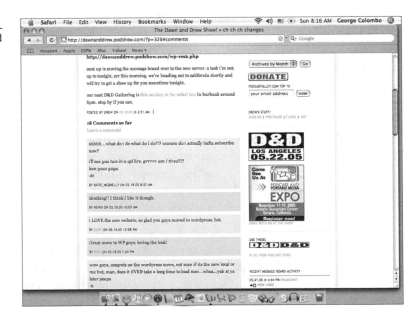

BLOGGING SOFTWARE FOR YOUR WEBSITE

If you're maintaining your podcast's web presence on a blogging site such as blogger.com then you're all set. If, on the other hand, you're maintaining your own website and want to add blogging capabilities to it, that's easy to do.

WordPress is open-source software that's available for free and can be easily installed on your website. Some web hosting companies offer WordPress installation as a free option with their web hosting services. If yours is one of them, and you didn't install WordPress with your initial installation, you can still add it on at any time. If your web host doesn't offer WordPress, check to see if it supports PHP (the scripting language of WordPress) and MySQL. Most hosts offer these, although some do so more elegantly than others. If you're not confident in your host's capabilities, ask for links to a few sites they're hosting that already have WordPress installed. Once you've determined that your web host can accommodate your needs, you can download WordPress for free at wordpress.org and install it yourself.

Once it's installed, WordPress makes it easy for you to post your show notes (although a basic knowledge of HTML will make things considerably easier). It also automatically provides for listener comments and gives you options for moderating those comments. If you have programming skills, you can modify the appearance of your WordPress website yourself. Otherwise, there are dozens of WordPress templates—available for free online—that can do the job for you.

Many of the most popular podcasts use WordPress to power their websites. Go to the home page of your favorite podcast and scroll down to the bottom. Chances are good that you'll find a small notice there specifying that the site runs on WordPress.

Email Strategies

Another important mechanism for getting feedback from your listeners is email. Email is more personal than feedback posted on a website. As a result, it capitalizes on the personal connection that your listeners feel with your podcast.

Email is also more private than posting on your website. Many listeners will feel reluctant to post a message that anyone who visits your site can read.

Any email address will be fine for providing basic email functionality, including an email address associated with your domain. Lately, however, many podcasters have opted instead to use Google's free email service, Gmail. One reason for this is the fact that Gmail provides an enormous amount of storage with each Gmail account, an important consideration if you're soliciting audio comments (see the following section). However, the amount of available storage isn't the only reason you should consider opening a Gmail account.

Gmail automatically categorizes your mail into "conversations." All related mail is organized so that you can follow a thread of correspondence, even if several people are involved. This organization works in conjunction with Google's legendary search technology. The result is that Gmail makes it much easier for you to find patterns in the feedback you get from listeners.

Accepting Audio Feedback

As we mentioned a moment ago, there's one other key benefit to using Gmail: The fact that Gmail provides you with an enormous amount of storage capacity. If you were simply a regular user, that would still be important since it means you can leave all your email on the Gmail server and access it from any computer that's connected to the Internet.

As a podcaster, though, the amount of storage Gmail provides has a special significance. That storage allows you to conveniently use Gmail to receive audio feedback.

What's audio feedback? It's when, instead of writing down his or her feedback, a listener records it and then sends it to you as an audio file. For other types of online content providers, audio feedback doesn't comprise a significant amount of the total feedback they receive. It's different for you as a podcaster, though. You are far more likely than, say, a blogger to get feedback in the form of an audio file.

There's nothing surprising about this, when you think about it. Podcast listeners are savvy when it comes to digital media and are often aspiring podcasters themselves. It's only natural that they would be inclined to send you audio files.

Feedback from audio files is highly desirable for a few reasons:

■ Someone in your audience taking the time to provide audio feedback is a sign that you're really connecting with your listeners. People wouldn't do this if they didn't care about your show.

■ Audio feedback provides emphasis and inflection you don't get from email.

■ You can use clips from your audio feedback in your podcast!

By all means, encourage your listeners to send you their audio feedback. And if you're using a Gmail account, you'll have more than enough storage to save and conveniently access all the files you receive.

By the way, in addition to show feedback, there are a few other types of audio files your listeners might occasionally send in, depending on the kind of show you produce:

■ Intros for your show

■ Promos for their show

■ Podsafe music

Your Gmail account is a great place to receive and store all of these.

Show Feedback Line

Just about everything we discussed concerning audio feedback applies to a show feedback phone number, too. A show feedback line consists of a phone line that's connected to voice mail, allowing a listener to simply say what's on his or her mind. Like audio feedback, phone lines produce high-quality feedback that, as an added bonus, you can use in your show.

The advantage of a show feedback line for your listeners is that it's more immediate and convenient than recording their own audio feedback. All they have to do is pick up a phone, call you, and leave their feedback at the sound of the tone! Some podcasts use regular land or cellular lines for their feedback. Increasingly, some are also using Skype Voicemail (which we'll be discussing in more detail in a moment) or some combination of the two, as you can see in Figure 5.4.

FIGURE 5.4

The Cubicle Escape Pod gives listeners the option of leaving show feedback on a regular phone line or via Skype Voicemail.

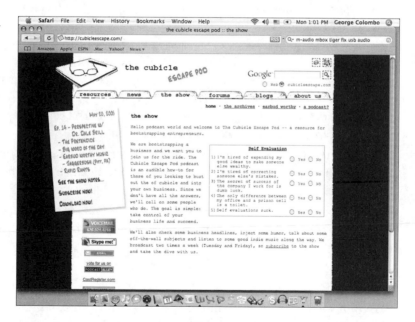

The only disadvantage to maintaining a show feedback line is the cost. If you're maintaining a dedicated line, it can cost $35.00 per month or more. As of this writing, an annual subscription to Skype Voicemail costs 15 Euros. That's much less expensive than a phone line but it is inaccessible to any listeners who don't use Skype.

Skype

Skype provides telephone service over the Internet, a technology that's also known as *Voice over IP (VoIP)*. Skype is different from the other companies in this market in one important respect: It's free.

At least, the software is free. And when one Skype user is talking to another, all the talk time is free, too. That's true, by the way, for users all over the world. You can talk to other Skype users anywhere in the world for as long as you'd like for without paying a cent (as long as you're both using Skype).

If free isn't persuasive enough, there's another reason why you should be familiar with Skype. Since conversations over Skype take place over the Internet, they are already in digital format. It's relatively easy, then, to turn that digital conversation into an audio file for your podcast. As a result, the majority of podcasts that feature remote conversations use Skype to do so.

Whatever audio equipment you're using for your podcast is probably fine for Skype, although if you have a headset laying around, that's probably going to be the most convenient option. Go to www.skype.com and select the Download button from the Home page. You'll be taken to a screen that allows you to select your software platform. Operating system options are Windows 2000 or XP, Macintosh OS X, Linux, and Pocket PC.

Select your operating system of choice and your download will begin. Once you've downloaded Skype, follow the onscreen instructions for installation. Select a screen name and a password, and you're in business. Skype works very much like instant messenger software—in fact, it has instant messaging built in. You can create a Contacts list that will allow you to see other Skype users. Even more important, you can allow other Skype users to see when you're online.

Let your listeners know that they should feel free to contact you when you're online. Feedback that you get on your show that's live and interactive can be the best feedback of all.

One final caveat: If you're going to use clips from audio feedback in your podcast, then Skype can be difficult to work with depending on the software you use to produce your show.

And Furthermore...

Now that we've reviewed the various tools at your disposal, it's important to understand a few additional principles about getting and using feedback from your listeners:

Offer Your Listeners Multiple Options for Providing Feedback

You probably have a friend who just doesn't use email. If this individual has something to tell you, he will almost always pick up a phone instead of sitting down and writing a note. Conversely, you probably also have a friend who never calls but sends you several emails a day. And, if you think about it, you'll probably be able to point to one or two quirks in your own communication style. In fact, we all have idiosyncrasies when it comes to our communication style.

Your listeners are exactly the same way. Some prefer voice communications, some prefer written communications, and some will bounce back and forth between the two depending on the situation. The important point for you to remember, then, is to make sure you offer your listeners as many choices as possible when they want to communicate with you. We'll examine each of your options in a moment but, in the meantime, simply note that you're better off when you offer as many alternatives as possible.

When you limit feedback options, you're skewing the nature of your responses in ways that are difficult to predict and impossible to compensate for. It's a variation of the issue faced by pollsters in the 2004 U.S. election: Younger voters were far more likely than older voters to rely on cell phones rather than traditional land lines. Polling organizations that relied solely on phone polls had a tough time putting representative data together.

The bottom line? Make sure you offer multiple options for listener feedback. Follow the example of the *this WEEK in TECH* podcast, as shown in Figure 5.5, which offers several feedback options.

FIGURE 5.5

This popular podcast allows listeners to offer feedback via email, audio files, voice mail, and fax.

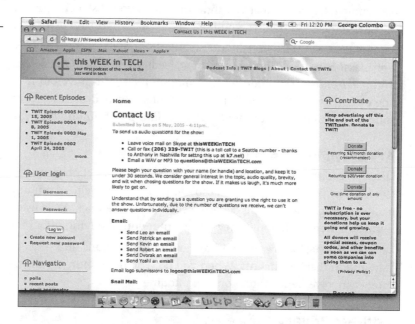

Solicit Feedback, Not Flattery

When you first launch your podcast—before you've had a chance to promote or publicize it with the techniques you'll learn about in Chapter 11, "Promoting Your Podcast"—most of the feedback you'll receive will be from friends and family. When you ask them for feedback about your podcast, it's only natural that they'll try to be as positive and supportive as possible. That impulse is understandable but, unfortunately, it's just not helpful.

Assure this early group of listeners that you're not one of the folks W. Somerset Maugham was referring to when he observed, "People ask for criticism, but they only want praise." Let them know that the best way to support your efforts is to be candid about what's working and what's not.

When you're getting feedback from family and friends, ask for specific examples of what they like and what they don't. "Your podcast—is that what you call it? A podcast?—was very nice," may be gratifying but it's not a helpful response.

Put the Feedback You Receive into Its Proper Perspective

A pollster who looked at all the methods we discussed for getting feedback from your listeners would tell you to be very careful drawing conclusions from what you hear. The problem is that everyone who's giving you feedback is self-selected. There's no convenient way of knowing if this group of people is representative of your entire audience.

As a practical matter, what does that mean? Well, for one thing, you probably know that people who are angry with you or critical of something you've said are a great deal more likely to contact you than the rest of your listeners who agree with you. Those listeners might agree and they might not. There's no great way of knowing.

So, if feedback is self-selected and potentially unrepresentative, does that mean it's worthless? Not at all. It means that the feedback you get isn't determinative of anything *all by itself*. It's important information for you to have but it's only one guideline out of several that you'll use to evaluate your podcast. Get as much input as you can but understand that it's just one data point among many.

Acknowledge Receiving Feedback

Listener feedback creates its own momentum. If you acknowledge receiving listener feedback in your podcasts—and especially if you play clips from any audio feedback you might get—you'll generate even more feedback. Your listeners will communicate more with you if they believe that you're paying attention.

Let your listeners know that you're reading their emails and posts and that you're listening to their comments. When you do, you'll get more feedback—and more listener involvement—than you can imagine.

Address Privacy Concerns

For a variety of reasons, it's a good idea to develop a set of policies for your website about privacy issues, then clearly communicate those policies to your listeners. The most important policy you'll want to formulate has to do with any email addresses or personal information that's posted to your site or conveyed to you via email. If your policy is to never sell, rent, or otherwise disseminate email addresses—as it probably should be—then say so. Conversely, if there's any chance of your ever using that information in a commercial context, then it's important to let listeners know that up front.

Along the same lines, if you're going to publicly use any of the feedback you receive, you'll want to let listeners know that before they contact you. A listener whose audio feedback turns up in one of your podcasts might be thrilled to be quoted. Or he might not. At the very least, you will want to communicate up front that the possibility exists and provide an opportunity to opt out.

THE ABSOLUTE MINIMUM

Here what you need to know about connecting with your listeners and creating a positive feedback loop:

- Creating a podcast that connects with your listeners is easier when you're getting regular feedback from them.

- A blog for your show notes is your most important tool for connecting with your listeners.

- Email needs to be a fundamental component of your feedback strategy.

- Audio feedback—via audio clips, voice mail messages on your show's voice mail system, and interactive conversations on Skype—is a high-quality, high-impact way to interact with your listeners.

6

SETTING UP YOUR STUDIO

Making a podcast means setting up a recording studio—even if the studio is on your kitchen table! In this chapter, you'll learn the basic ingredients of a recording studio and how they work together. You'll discover that you don't need to spend a lot of money to set up a basic recording studio, and that paying attention to a couple of key components can make a huge difference in the way your podcast sounds. We'll also take you out of the studio to record your podcast "in the field," and you'll see that, once you've developed a basic toolkit and some essential skills, there's practically no limit to where you can create a winning podcast.

The Hardware and Accessories You'll Need

When it comes to recording, you need components to take care of a handful of jobs: You need something to turn sound into electrical signals; something to record those electrical signals into a digital file; a way to listen to your recording to make sure it sounds the way you want it to; and cables to move signals between all these other components. For most of us, the pieces we use for these jobs will be a microphone, a computer, headphones, and cables. Most of the time, it's easy to make sure that all of the pieces work well together, but there are a few key issues to watch for when you're choosing components to make sure you avoid problems when you're building your studio.

Table 6.1   Equipment You'll Need to Begin Podcasting

Component	Purpose
Hardware	
Computer	Holds everything together
Sound Card	Converts analog sound wave to digital sound files (and back again)—provides physical connection between microphone and computer
Microphone	Converts sound pressure waves to electrical signals
Cable	Carries electrical signal between components
Headphones	Allow a person to listen to podcasts without annoying others
Mixing Board	Combines the signals from two or more microphones (or other sound sources) into a single signal for recording
Software	
Recording Software	Controls the process of recording a sound file on your computer
Editing/Mixing Software	Allows you to make changes in recorded sound files or combine multiple sound files into a single file
FTP Software	File Transfer Protocol software for moving completed sound files from your computer to the server where others will find them
Accessories	
Portable Recorders	For making recordings when you can't have a computer with you
Cases	You want to keep your studio safe when you take it on the road
Cameras	For documenting the visual landscape when you're recording your podcast

One of the first places you'll want to pay attention to is in the selection of "professional" equipment versus "consumer" equipment. Now, there are pieces of your setup where this doesn't matter at all—your choice of headphones, for example. Whether you buy your headphones from a huge retailer or a recording-industry supplier, the headphones will work the same (though there can be huge differences in the quality of the sound). On the other end of the process, microphones are a component where the difference between professional and consumer equipment can be huge.

We'll go into more detail on some differences later in this chapter, but the basic rule is this: You can generally connect professional components into consumer components successfully if you pay attention to your volume controls; professional equipment tends to operate at higher voltages (which translate into higher volume levels) than consumer equipment. That voltage difference makes it difficult to plug consumer equipment into professional equipment with any success—the volume level of the consumer equipment tends to come across as so low that the professional gear doesn't pick it up.

> **tip**
>
> Can't tell whether a microphone (or other piece of gear) is pro or consumer? Look at the operating rating. If the device is listed as operating at "+4 dBm" or "+4dBu" then it's almost certainly professional gear. If it operates at "–10 dBV line level" then it's consumer gear. From an electrical perspective, the pro equipment operates with its reference, or 0 dB level, at 1.228 volts, while the consumer gear has its reference, or 0 dB level, at 0.316 volts. That voltage difference is much of the explanation for why it can be difficult to combine pro and consumer gear in certain ways.

Choosing a Computer Platform: Windows, Macintosh, or Linux

Okay, so we'll start by admitting that most people already have chosen a computer operating system, so you won't need our help on this score. We'll also point out that software is available for Windows, Macintosh, and Linux systems that will let you put together a spectacular podcast. We'll get into the specifics for that software a little bit later in this chapter. What follows, then, is a discussion for those who are trying to decide whether to switch from one operating system to another, or for folks who just want to feel superior about the choice they've already made.

Windows

If you want a platform that has a wide array of recording, editing, and posting options, with the range in quality varying widely, as well, then Microsoft Windows should be at the top of your list. More specifically, Windows XP should be at the top of your list. There are many programs out there for the various tasks, with prices ranging from free to hundreds of dollars, and while most do their thing in a unique way, all are tied together through the Windows graphical user interface.

The hardware that Windows runs on can be quite inexpensive, with new systems often on sale for as little as $300. There are three things you'll want to think about when buying Windows software, though, and they all have to do with the nature of sound files. Windows's native audio format is the .WAV file, which tends to be much larger than MP3 files for the same recording. You'll want as much RAM as you can afford in your system—you should consider 512 megabytes the minimum, and go for a gigabyte (or more) if at all possible. The same issues should drive your choice of hard disk and CD-/DVD-ROM drives. Maintaining a library of audio recordings will eat up a good deal of hard disk real estate, so plan to buy as much storage as you can afford. Since even the smallest of podcasting files is unlikely to fit on a floppy disk, you should plan on getting a CD-R or DVD-R drive in your system to back up your files (and you'll want to back up your files).

The last thing you should consider is your sound card. Most desktop and laptop PCs come with a sound card, but the standard sound card may not provide the kind of quality you want in your podcast. Investing in a high-quality sound card can make an immediate difference in the quality of your recordings. Most of the higher-quality sound cards now support surround sound, which won't matter to your podcast, but the ability to handle the high-demand surround sound usually indicates that the circuits that convert between analog sound and digital files (and back again) are of higher quality.

Macintosh

The Apple Macintosh is the computer that many people think of when the topic is audio or video creation and it is, in fact, the wonderful interface and reputation that keep the Macintosh at the top of the consideration list. There are not quite as many freeware and shareware packages available for the Mac as there are for the PC, but many of the existing software packages are genuinely quite well integrated and easy to use with minimal training.

Some people feel that the Macintosh is overpriced, but there are models that are competitive with essentially any Windows computer currently being sold on the market. The Mac is not fully competitive with the lowest-end PCs, but the Mac Mini and various iMacs are inexpensive and capable platforms for very little money.

Linux

Linux is growing in popularity because of its low cost and increasingly easy user experience. While many people associate Linux with hackers and computer experts, it's now possible to use Linux with no more depth of computer knowledge than is required for Windows.

Since the hardware platforms for Linux and Windows are often the same, the considerations tend to be the same, as well. The biggest difference regards sound cards, and is the question of drivers—the very basic software that tells the operating system what to do with the digital information coming from the device. Linux drivers are available for most of the popular sound cards, and more become available each month, but you should check to make sure that a driver is available before you buy a particular sound card for your Linux system

Headphones

Headphones are important because they let you listen to your podcast as most of your listeners will hear the recording. There are three basic types of headphones—in-ear, open-ear, and isolation—and each will color the sound that you hear when you listen to the podcast. There are two reasons why you should care about the differences in headphone sound, and both of them deal with how well your listener will be able to understand and enjoy your podcast.

The first difference between headphones is the amount of outside, or "room" noise they allow in when you're listening to a recording. The second is whether the sound reproduction of the headphone leans toward sounds that are higher or lower in pitch. Together, these two characteristics will affect what your listeners think of the quality of your podcast.

Closed-ear (Isolation) Headphones

Isolation headphones (the classic "ear muff" headphones) allow relatively little noise to come in to blend with the sound of the recording and will tend to produce sound that's heavier on bass tones than the other types of headphones. While most recording artists and audio engineers use these headphone (which they call "cans") while in the studio, they have two disadvantages that may be important for you; they will isolate you from your surroundings, and they are hot to wear for any length of time. If you're mixing a podcast while wearing cans, be aware that listeners using the other types of headphones may find your mix lighter on bass, or more tinny-sounding, than you intend.

Open-ear Headphones

Open-ear headphones typically have the least bass boost and allow in far more room noise. If you're putting together a podcast with music (especially club or rock music), and edit a final version that has plenty of bass, or if you equalize a spoken voice (especially a male voice) to have a particularly deep tone in your open-ear headphones, the recording may end up sounding "muddy" if someone with isolation headphones starts listening.

In-ear Headphones

In-ear headphones have the greatest variation in sound among headphone types, though almost all share the quality of blocking significant noise from outside. Most offer very good reproduction through the middle of the sound spectrum, where the human voice tends to be found. The best of this type, which can cost $400 or more, can have quite extraordinary sound quality. The downside for many people is the comfort factor—a lot of folks just don't like to have something stuck in their ears.

When you choose a headset, the most important factor is comfort. If you start building complex podcasts, you may be wearing headphones for extended periods of time, and you want to be able to concentrate on your show, rather than the uncomfortable headphones. If the sound quality is important to you, try to listen to your podcast, at least occasionally, with headphones other than your main set, so you can make sure that you're not mixing at a level of sound quality that works with your main headphones alone.

Microphones

The sound of your podcast really begins with your microphone. Microphones convert vibrations traveling through the air into electrical signals that your computer can understand. There are several ways to do this, and we'll look at what the different methods mean for the way the microphone sounds. First, though, we'll learn about the two sets of descriptions you'll see used for the microphones you consider.

The first set of descriptions talks about the way that the microphone works; how the sound becomes electricity. Most of the words you'll see are dynamic, condenser, and electret. We'll look at what these words mean in a couple of paragraphs. There are other types, including carbon, ribbon, and pressure response, but you're much less likely to need to run across them in podcasting.

The next set of descriptions focuses on how the microphone is used, and where the microphone should be in relation to your mouth. Omni-directional, cardioid, shotgun, lavalier, and parabolic are the terms we'll be visiting in a few short paragraphs.

Dynamic Microphones

Most microphones work, in some way, like a speaker in reverse. Where a speaker shakes a diaphragm, using vibrations to produce sound, microphones allow vibrations to shake a diaphragm in order to capture sound. In a dynamic microphone, the diaphragm is connected to a coil of wire. The coil either surrounds or is next to one or more magnets. As the diaphragm makes the coil move in the magnetic field, a changing electric current is generated, and that current is translated into the sound file that can be stored.

FIGURE 6.1

Dynamic mics convert vibrations into changes in a magnetic field, which generates changing voltages that are recorded as sound.

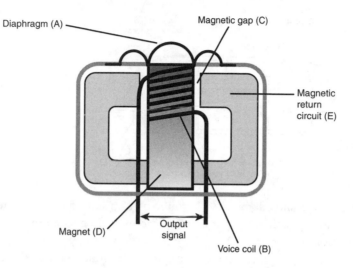

Dynamic mics are nice because they don't require an additional, external power source in order to operate. The downside is that it takes (relatively speaking) a lot of vibration to move the coil enough to register a sound. That means that dynamic mics aren't the most sensitive microphones you'll find, but they are pretty tough to destroy; a high wind (or exceptionally loud noise) that might damage a sensitive condenser microphone is much less likely to harm your sturdy dynamic mic.

Condenser Microphones

In a condenser mic, the diaphragm is given an electrical charge and placed next to a flat plate that has an opposite electrical charge. As the diaphragm moves toward and away from the plate, a changing electrical current is generated. Now, this current is much weaker than that generated by a dynamic mic, so there has to be a small amplifier (or "pre-amplifier") in the microphone to make the signal strong enough to make it all the way to the rest of the equipment.

It doesn't take much of a vibration to start the weak current flowing, so a condenser mic can be very, very sensitive. Most of the microphones used in commercial recording studios and radio stations are condenser mics. In these very controlled environments, the biggest limitation of the condenser mic isn't an issue; most condenser microphones require an outside electrical source to charge the diaphragm and plate, and to power the pre-amp. Most commercial recording equipment can provide this electricity through a service called "phantom power" that's available on some or all of the microphone input jacks on the equipment.

Some condenser mics, especially those that are less expensive, use a chemical process (applied at the factory) to generate the electrical charge required to make the microphone work. These mics, called *electret* microphones, don't require the external power source, though they trade some sensitivity for the flexibility. Most small portable microphones, like those used on video cameras, computer headsets, or portable recorders, are electret mics.

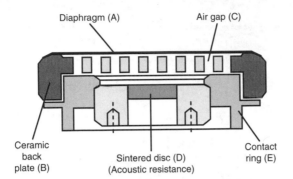

FIGURE 6.2
The diaphragm
and charged
plate of the
condenser mic
make it more
sensitive than
the dynamic
microphone.

So which type should you buy? If you're getting started and want to use the microphone that's attached to your headset, then you'll be using an electret mic, and that's okay. If your podcast is going to involve taking your recording studio around to lots of different places, then your first microphone upgrade should be to a good dynamic mic because it will sound good and stand up to the rigors of being thrown around in a field bag or backpack. The condenser mic? When sound quality is the only consideration and you've moved up to an all-professional recording studio, then you'll be ready to shell out for the condenser that comes in its own wooden box and makes you sound like a million dollars.

Microphone Patterns

If recording your podcast involves you and a microphone then the pattern won't really matter all that much. If you're going to be recording a group of people, recording things that aren't right next to the microphone, or trying to limit the extra "noise" that gets into the microphone then the pattern starts to matter a great deal.

The first pattern you may hear about is omni-directional. Omni-directional mics pick up sound equally well no matter where the source sits in relation to the microphone. This is great if you're trying to record a group of people, or if you don't want to have to worry about precisely where the microphone is, but it's not so good if you want the microphone to help eliminate noise that exists in the room, or if you want to pick up sound that is far away from the mic in a particular direction.

A cardioid pattern is, as its name implies, somewhat heart-shaped. This means that there is one direction in which the microphone is most sensitive—which usually translates into being able to pick up sound at a greater distance in that direction. Greater sensitivity in one direction means less sensitivity in the others, so unwanted noise doesn't make it into the recording quite as much as with omni-directional microphones.

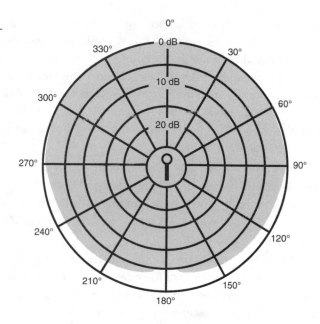

FIGURE 6.3
Your direction to the microphone doesn't matter with an omni-directional pattern.

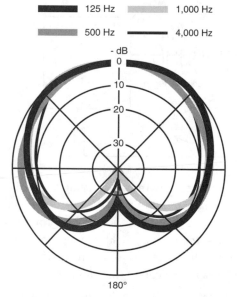

FIGURE 6.4
The cardioid pattern extends much farther in one direction.

	125 Hz		1,000 Hz
	500 Hz		4,000 Hz

Cables

The home stereo industry has worked very hard to convince people that they simply must have cables made of precious metals, created by exotic processes, in order to get good sound. You might think that the same is true of recording, but for podcasting, the fact is that some very simple, low-cost cables will work perfectly well to carry your recording from place to place.

Now, let's stop for a moment to state, without question, that there are differences in cables, and that those differences can have an effect on the sound that goes into a recording. For most podcasters, though, the sound difference that comes from a top-of-the-line cable versus a good cable will be masked by the limitations of the microphone, the sound card, or the encryption rate you select for your MP3 file. We recommend that you choose good cables—those in the middle of the price range—but that you not obsess over the quality of a component that doesn't have the greatest effect on the sound of your podcast.

The biggest difference that you're likely to see in your cables comes from the connector type and the words "balanced" or "unbalanced." Both of these issues tend to pop up when you start mixing professional equipment with consumer components. Now, we'll take a look at when you might see those differences, and what you should do about them as a podcaster.

Let's start with balanced and unbalanced cables. If you're using the cable that's already connected to a microphone (like the one on a headset or a low-cost lavalier mic) then you're using unbalanced cable. This means that there are two wires, each one carrying audio signal, and no separate grounding conductor.

FIGURE 6.5

There is no separate ground on an unbalanced cable.

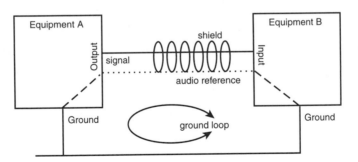

A balanced cable has three conductors, with two carrying the audio signal and one (often a braided-metal wrapper surrounding the other two wires) that is dedicated to providing the ground. Why is the ground important? A grounded system is better at keeping noise out of the line—the hums, crackles, pops, and assorted sonic gremlins—that can detract from the substance of the recording. The more sensitive your microphones, and the longer your cables, the more this matters.

Now, here's the big thing to remember about balanced and unbalanced cables: If you're working with the type of cables and microphones you're going to find in most computer stores, you'll be using all unbalanced cables, and that's okay. You'll need to think about balanced cables when one of the following things happens:

■   You buy a professional microphone. Professional mics tend to have XLR connectors (like the one in Figure 6.7). XLR cables are generally balanced. If you need to connect your XLR microphone to a piece of equipment that has sockets for 1/4" or 1/8" phone plugs (like the one in Figure 6.8), then buy a cable that has the two necessary connectors, rather than a bunch of adapters; you'll be much happier with the sound quality.

FIGURE 6.6

A balanced cable has a separate ground conductor.

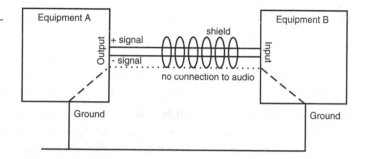

FIGURE 6.7

The XLR connector has three separate signal pins.

■ You start to move to professional equipment. If you have a mix of professional and consumer gear, with their combination of balanced and unbalanced circuits, then it's time to purchase some adapter components (grounding boxes, rather than cable adapters) to put in line. By the time you're ready for this step, you're past the "Absolute Beginner's" stage, and we'll trust you to someone else's expertise.

FIGURE 6.8

The phone connector has two or three signals on a single shaft.

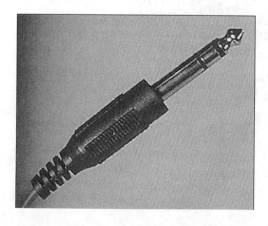

One of the components you're likely to buy as you begin to build more sophisticated podcasts is a mixing board—a way to use several microphones or inputs to make everything sound great.

A Mixing Board

A mixing board is, to many people, the symbol of a "real" recording studio. At its most basic, this is a tool that lets you take multiple microphones (or other sound sources) and route them to a single output. For podcasters, a mixing board can be the route to giving everyone in an interview situation their own microphone.

When you start looking at mixing boards, you'll see input counts ranging from 2 to 64. You'll see small metal boxes with one knob, and huge consoles with phalanxes of sliders, knobs, switches, and meters. Fortunately, for podcasting, your mixing needs are modest and the equipment required is simple.

If you want to have multiple microphones, plan to keep the count to six or less, and buy only as much mixing board as you need. If you truly need phantom power for a condenser microphone, XLR sockets, a mix of balanced and unbalanced inputs, and multiple meters for monitoring the level of each input channel, then by all means get them. If, on the other hand, you simply need a way to get four microphones mixed into a single output that goes into your sound card for recording, then you should be able to find a mixing board for $100 or less that will give you what you need.

FIGURE 6.9

A small six-channel mixer can be found for less than $100.

Choosing a mixer that has only the features you need has several advantages. They tend to be less expensive; they are easier to learn how to use; and they are smaller, allowing them to be more easily carried if you want to move your recording out of your studio and into the field.

Recording in the Field

One of the great things about podcasts is that they can be created anywhere. With some simple tools and basic techniques, you can record a podcast in the park or the local coffeehouse as easily as in your studio. With a headset microphone plugged into your laptop computer's sound card, the world is your studio! We have recorded simple podcasts in airports, on airplanes, in conference rooms, and on the back porch. The real fun, though, comes when you want to take advantage of your remote location's unique qualities, rather than merely creating a standard podcast from a non-standard location.

When you get out of the studio, you really begin to take your listeners to places they couldn't go without your help. Rather than simply telling them about a street festival, you can let them walk along with you, hearing the sounds of the crowds and vendors, and talking to the artists and neighborhood leaders who put the festival together. Instead of reading the names of the winners at the Friday night dirt-track races, you can take them into the stands to hear the roar of the engines and the thump of dirt clods landing around you—and you can ask people in the stands who they're rooting for and why they come to the races every week.

Moving your podcast into the field changes the basic dynamic of the recording and the experience you create for your listeners. While great content is still the most critical ingredient in a successful podcast, using the right tools and techniques are the equivalent of a writer's well chosen words—they can make the experience dramatically more vibrant, immediate, and real for those listening to the podcast.

Your headset mic and laptop soundcard can allow you to record a vocal track in spite of a remote location. Working with remote locations can take a different approach to recording, and a different set of tools. In many remote sites, for example, a laptop computer is too large and unwieldy to make a useful recorder. If you'll be standing or walking around with your recorder in your hands, for instance, a laptop computer is almost impossible. In the same way, if going "on location" involves talking with other people for your podcast, the headset microphone loses in efficiency far more than it gains in enforced intimacy.

As with your studio setup, you'll need a recording device, a microphone, and a way to listen to your recorded piece. Depending on the specifics of the situation, you might want a way to edit your recording, ways to insulate the microphone from the environment, and a camera and notebook to document the session. If remote recording is something you'll do more than once or twice, you'll also want some way to carry your studio around.

It's worth taking a moment to talk about your carrying case; you want something that protects your equipment, is easy to carry, and won't come between you and what you want to record. Depending on your equipment, you might choose something as small as a waist pouch or lumbar pack: a bag designed to carry 35mm camera equipment can be ideal (see Figure 6.10). You might, on the other hand, choose a backpack with partitions you've cut out of high-density foam to organize and protect your gear. Regardless of the case you choose, make sure that the contents are protected against the shocks, drops, and insults of the real world.

FIGURE 6.10

Carrying cases for your portable studio can range from small, inexpensive waist pouches to full-sized hardshell backpacks.

As with virtually every aspect of podcasting, there are many options for each of these pieces, depending on how much money you want to spend and which aspects of field recording are most important to you. Let's take a look at the pieces you can use to build your portable podcasting studio.

Portable Recorders

Portable recorders for podcasts can take many forms, depending on the criteria that are most important to you. Does small size trump all other considerations? Is it important that your portable recorder perform other tasks? Are you looking to create audio documentaries that feature the highest-quality sound quality? A "Yes" answer to each of these questions leads down a different path for a possible recorder.

Pocket Recorders

Many pocket recorders, of the sort doctors and executives use to dictate notes and memos, generate sound files that can be downloaded to a personal computer through a USB or FireWire cable. When it comes to pure portability, this is the champion, as many models from Panasonic, Minolta, or Sony are comparable in size to small cell phones. The small size is often accompanied by very long recording times, and models that include four, six, or more hours of recording time are common.

Digital voice recorders also tend to be inexpensive, with models starting around $50.00 and going up to around $250.00. While the combination of small size and low price might make these seem the perfect all-around answer, this class of recorder tends to have a couple of limitations that take it out of consideration for many podcasters.

In order to achieve the long recording time, most pocket voice recorders sample at a low rate, providing a recorded voice that is perfectly intelligible but which lacks the quality heard in larger recorders. This is compounded by the microphones built into these machines, mics that are optimized to pick up the average human voice. It sounds like a good idea until you listen and discover that voices that are quite high or very deep don't record with the richness we'd like, and that ambient sounds—the sounds that let the listener get a feeling for where we're recording—may not record realistically at all. Pocket recorders are great "just in case" devices that you can keep in your pocket, purse, or briefcase for spontaneous interviews, or as backups for a more capable system should something break in the field. For most podcasters, though, the quality of the recording made with a pocket recorder won't match the quality of the content.

> **tip**
>
> The reduced sound quality of a pocket recorder can add to the "live" feeling of a field interview when it's contrasted against a studio-recorded intro and wrap-up. Make sure, though, that the quality of your recording is good enough to not get in the way of your content.

FIGURE 6.11

The pocket recorder (left) is the most portable recording option. The MiniDisc recorder (right) brings higher quality at a significantly higher cost.

MiniDisc Recorders

MiniDisc recorders are one step up from the pocket recorders in size, and a quantum leap ahead in potential sound quality. With the 160 megabyte storage space of a MiniDisc that provides about 74 minutes in audio mode, these players can record at a much higher sampling rate than is possible with the smaller handheld devices. Unfortunately, MiniDisc players, which some observers believed would take over from both standard audiocassette records and CD players, are considerably more expensive than most pocket recorders, with prices in the $200–$600 range. Many MiniDisc players, such as the one shown in Figure 6.11, have a built-in microphone that may be of little better quality than those found in pocket recorders. With a high-quality external microphone, though, they can be very acceptable field recording choices. Journalists tend to like MiniDisc recorders very much, though their lack of mass-market acceptance can make the recorders and their disks a little hard to find in some markets.

MP3 Player with Recorder

If multi-purpose devices are your requirement, then your MP3 player may be an ideal solution. Some MP3 players, such as those from Creative Labs, iRiver, and Sony, have microphones and recording menus built-in. As with so many small devices, the quality of the built-in microphone will limit the ultimate quality of the recording, and players with smaller memories will be significantly limited in total recording time. Players that will accept an external mic, however, can be used to make very good recordings, and are being used by many successful podcasters. Even Apple iPods can be used as field recording devices with the addition of a small accessory that includes a microphone, external mic jack, and circuitry to provide input to the iPod through its accessory jack. There's a nice symmetry to using an MP3 player to record a podcast, though many users will find the user interface less than acceptable for recording jobs that involve any complexity at all.

Portable Multi-track Recorders

For podcasters who value recording quality and editing flexibility above other concerns, a portable multi-track recorder from a company such as Zoom, Korg, or Tascam is the answer. These portable studios, designed for traveling musicians to record song ideas and demos, will feature input jacks for commercial-quality microphones, high-quality audio conversion and digitizing circuits, and the ability to mix multiple recorded sources into a single final file. Depending on how important portability is, devices with various capabilities are available in sizes ranging from paperback book to large laptop computer, with the number of tracks, on-board storage capacity, control size, and simultaneous input circuits increasing with device size. An average-sized unit, balancing portability and functionality, is shown in Figure 6.12. If recording remote podcasts is a serious interest of yours, you'll want to look seriously at a portable multi-track recorder for the ultimate in quality and flexibility.

FIGURE 6.12

An MP3 player (left) can record interviews in the field. A portable multi-track recorder (right) is tops in recording quality and flexibility.

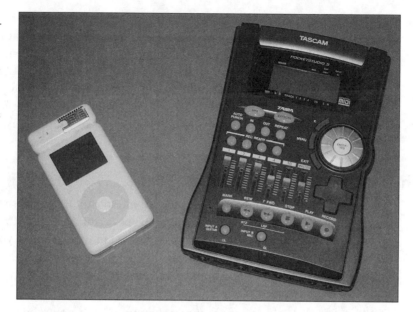

Accessories for Field Recording

Just as with recording in your studio, there are things you'll want to do to make sure that unintentional noises and artifacts don't get in the way of your content, and that you're able to capture all the sound required to create a compelling podcast. Let's look at some of the accessories you'll want to keep in your bag to make your podcast content sparkle.

Whether you're recording in the great outdoors or a hushed conference room, wind is the enemy of good recording. You'll definitely want to make sure you've got a good windscreen (or two), made for your type and style of microphone, in your bag. If you're recording outdoors, make installing the windscreen part of your pre-recording checklist. Indoors, you'll still want the windscreen installed if you're going to using a handheld microphone that you move back and forth between yourself and interview subjects. While you will have experimented to learn the best distance and angle at which to approach the mic, your interview subjects aren't likely to have the same experience, and so are likely to move closer to the mic than is necessary. You can even out volume in editing, and a windscreen will help keep breathing noises off your recorded tracks.

tip

A reporter's notebook or stack of 3×5 index cards fits into your pocket and is critical for writing yourself notes about the location, interview subject information, and directions for editing when you get back to the studio.

The microphone-passing trick makes you look like a television journalist, but since no one on the listening side will be watching, that's not such a great benefit. Instead, try to have a microphone stand to minimize the thumps and bumps of microphone handling sounds in your recording. The stand may not be practical if you're walking around to record at various places, but small, tabletop stands are inexpensive (usually less than $10), have vibration-isolating rubber feet, and make a real difference when it comes to keeping the sounds of your fingers, rings, and clothing out of the recording.

Microphones for Field Recording

Depending on exactly what sounds you're trying to capture in your podcast, the same microphone used in your studio may be perfect in the field. It may be, on the other hand, that you need an entirely different set of mics to make your podcast happen.

The first situation that might lead you to a new microphone is trying to capture sounds that are several feet to many yards away from you. For this, you need a highly directional microphone; either a shotgun mic, or a parabolic reflector microphone, both of which are shown in Figure 6.13. If you've seen professional football games on television, you've probably seen someone standing on the sidelines holding what looks like a small television satellite dish. That dish is a parabolic reflector that reflects sound to a focal point where the microphone element sits. If you want to podcast on birdcalls, alligator grunts, or other natural sounds made by animals difficult to get close to, then a parabolic mic may be your only choice. Most parabolic mics are professional-grade equipment, so make sure that you've chosen a dynamic microphone (rather than a condenser) so that phantom power isn't an issue, and that you have the necessary cable adapters to connect the mic to your recorder. They can be expensive, and they're certainly not unobtrusive, but nothing matches them when it comes to pulling in the sound from distant sources.

tip

The range of frequencies picked up by a parabolic mic is directly related to its size. For handheld parabolics, that means a frequency range that makes it far more suitable for bird songs than for male human voices. Shotgun mics have a far wider dynamic range that makes them much more useful if you're trying to record people speaking.

If the source of your sound isn't quite so far away then a shotgun mic is your ticket. These long, skinny microphones (their shape looks rather like a shotgun barrel, hence the name) have a reception pattern that is the opposite of omnidirectional—it is very directional, and extends far from the end of the mic. Shotgun mics are sometimes used as the boom mics on film shoots, as the same pattern that pulls in distant sounds makes it less likely that they will pick up sounds from surrounding sources. Those same qualities make them common accessories for video cameras, and their popularity for this use makes less-expensive models relatively easy to find.

FIGURE 6.13

Parabolic mics (right) use a dynamic element with a parabolic reflector to capture sound across distances. A shotgun mic (below) uses a specially-designed element to do the same thing.

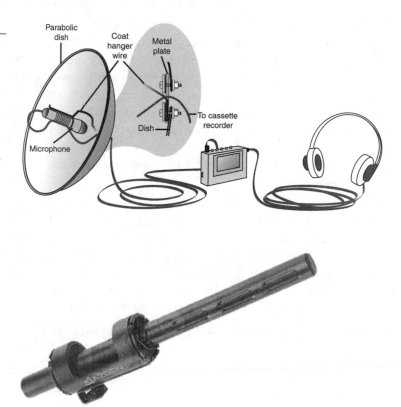

Shotgun mics come in a wide range of both price and quality. Those intended for film shoots can be hundreds of dollars (and weigh several pounds), while those aimed at the consumer market tend to cost less than a hundred dollars and weigh only a few ounces. Most podcasters will be more than happy with the consumer models, and the money saved compared to the professional models can be used to buy even more podcasting equipment.

Of course, it may well be that your studio mic is exactly what you need for recording your in-the-field podcast. The only true exception would be a ribbon microphone—while superb for vocal quality, the ribbon element is so fragile that a strong gust of wind can dislodge its seat and wreck the microphone. Both condenser and dynamic mics should be just fine, though, especially if you equip them with a windscreen before heading out to your session.

Windscreens

Here's the thing about the great outdoors: It's outside. That means that things like the wind become part of your studio. Since even a gentle breeze can produce a thundering roar in a microphone, a windscreen is an absolute must for in-the-field recording. There are many different windscreen types, and you can easily choose the best one to match your microphone and your needs.

The most common windscreens are simple foam wrappers that surround the microphone element housing. These can be very effective for gentle breezes, but they tend to be much less effective in even slightly stronger winds. You might be tempted to try saving money by wrapping a sheet of household foam packing material around the mic, and it's a trick that you can try in an emergency, but the acoustic qualities (how much sound they pass, and at what frequencies) of the packing foam are much different than those of the microphone windscreen. Foam windscreens aren't expensive (ranging from a few cents to a few dollars), and the sound quality is worth the money.

For stronger breezes and more sensitive shotgun mics, there are large fleece windscreens. These make your mic look vaguely like it's been swallowed by a sheep, but they are much more effective at cutting wind noise while maintaining the fidelity of the recording. These windscreens are frequently used in location shoots for film and television, and their cost reflects that professional association; they can cost from a few tens of dollar to well over $100, but if you've made the commitment to high-quality field recording equipment, they will be worth the money.

It's important to note that there are winds strong enough to make even the most expensive professional windscreens of little effect. When the zephyrs howl around you, it can be a sign that the time has come to work on in-studio podcasts—unless, that is, you're working on a "my time in a wind-tunnel" project.

Cameras

Okay, so a camera is not, strictly speaking, part of the equipment of a podcast. You're not going to use one to make a sound recording, and podcasts are about sound, right? Well, while a podcast is an audio activity, packaging, supporting, and documenting your podcast can take many forms. Photographs to aid in remembering who you've talked with, the situations about which you've podcasted, and the places in which you've recorded will make your podcasts, and the description on the website that surrounds the podcast, richer and more vibrant than they could be without the supporting material.

The nice thing about the camera required for documenting your podcast is that it doesn't have to be the same quality as a camera required for, say, scrapbooking or photojournalism. The resolution that's acceptable is that websites use a much lower resolution than is required for print. The resolution required for an image that appears on an MP3 player's screen to accompany your podcast may be even lower. These two viewing situations mean a small, inexpensive camera, such as the one in Figure 6.14 that tucks into your portable studio bag, is all you need to support the podcast.

FIGURE 6.14
The camera to document your podcasts can take up practically no room in your portable studio bag.

Many digital cameras come with video capabilities but, for most of us, they won't be necessary—all you need is the simple ability to put a basic image on your website to set the stage for your podcast. The level of expectation for the camera in this situation is low—and the price of the camera necessary to meet the expectation is similarly low.

When you take the role of the camera a bit further, you enter the realm of one of the more fascinating parts of podcasting—sound-seeing.

Working with Ambient Noise

Sound-seeing is taking the listener to a particular place at a specific time, allowing them to hear the sounds of a situation as though they were walking alongside you. Sound-seeing is all about making the most of the ambient sound, highlighting the aural landscape of a location to make the place seem real and immediate to your listener. In most cases, an omni-directional microphone is the best option because it "hears" sounds from nearly every direction, just as your ears do when you're walking through a location.

The difficulty can come when you're trying to narrate the ambient sounds as you present them. If you want to narrate as you're walking through the scene, you'll need to make sure that the microphone is close enough to you, and oriented properly, to ensure that the

tip

Recording your narration of the sound-seeing podcast in your studio gives you time to listen to the ambient sounds and plan what you will tell your listeners. It's easy to record the narration in pieces that refer to the photograph you post, the sound recording you've made, and links to other websites.

narration is louder than the ambient sounds, and distinct enough to be easily understood by the listener.

Since it can be difficult to walk around, narrate a podcast, watch relative levels, and monitor a recording all at the same time, you will probably want to record your narration after you've recorded the sound-seeing ambient tracks. This gives you the opportunity to think about what you've heard and record a great narration in your studio. You then get to edit the tracks together, using a program such as Audacity or Propoganda, adjusting the relative levels of the narration and ambient sounds for greatest impact and intelligibility.

Of course, sometimes you're recording in the field but you don't want to focus on the ambient sounds. It may be that you're trying to interview someone or focus on a particular sound, and you don't want to include every surrounding sound at the same level. In these situations you'll want to think about using a cardioid mic (for close-in vocals), or a shotgun or parabolic mic (for focusing on particular long-distance sounds).

FIGURE 6.15

Sound-seeing podcasts can give your listeners a real sense of a place—it's an exciting programming option to experiment with.

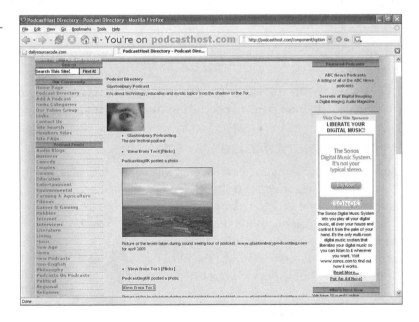

Regardless of how you decide to handle the ambient sounds, they are the critical component that separates field recordings from studio recordings. In the studio, ambient sounds are reduced to non-existence, while they are the critical component in a field recording. Learn to listen in 360 degrees, focusing attention on the sounds around you, as part of your preparation to take your podcast recording into the field. The result will be a podcast that's more interesting to far more people.

The Software You'll Need

To make all of this hardware work to build a podcast, you'll need software to tie everything together. The software will need to do several things: Record the basic files you'll want to build into a complete podcast; edit all the component files into your final program; and send the file from your computer to your server or podcast-hosting system. Let's look at the different software that's available for completing the various functions on different operating system platforms.

Recording Software

The first step in making your podcast is recording your words—the "glue" that will pull any music or sound-seeing files together, provide context, and make the result uniquely yours. The software must be able to take the audio from an input on your computer (most often the sound card, though the input could also be the USB [Universal Serial Bus] or FireWire [IEEE 1394] interface), control the sound level so that the resulting file is neither too soft nor too loud, and then write the recording to a file that can be used by the editing software to create the final podcast file. It's a straightforward set of actions, but on any platform there will be several products that make them possible.

The software that we'll be looking at is aimed at the beginner who's interested in podcasting. On all three platforms, there are high-end recording software packages available for professional and advanced amateurs who want to record music or the soundtrack for a film. These advanced packages are extraordinarily capable, and create the sort of recordings that you buy at the CD store, but require a high-powered computer and a serious investment in both time and money. The great news is that, for podcasting, the much more reasonable software we'll discuss will produce results that are just as good.

Macintosh Recording Software

Apple's Macintosh is the computer many people think of when audio and video come up. There are several pieces of software available for making recordings on the Macintosh. The first group is available for no money, for a donation, or for a very modest fee.

Audio Recorder 2.2 is freeware software that has a simple interface and simple functions for recording on the Macintosh. Its main competitor in the free software group is Audacity, the free recording package that's available for Macintosh, Windows, and Linux. Both Audio Recorder and Audacity are superb tools for making simple recordings, though you need to keep one thing in mind. For a variety of legal reasons, neither includes the native ability to create an MP3 file. In order to make MP3 files, you'll need to download and install the LAME framework, a free collection of libraries and functions that does nothing but enable MP3 creation. Once installed, you'll simply click on the menu items for exporting to or creating an MP3 file, and the conversion happens without further intervention.

Commercial Macintosh recording software starts with Apple's own GarageBand, software that was intended as a simple way for people to record music, but which works well for recording a basic podcast audio. One of the advantages of GarageBand is that so many people use it— it's easy to find user communities online to ask for help or get tips on the software. There are a pair of relatively minor disadvantages, as well. First, GarageBand was created for musicians, so there's a lot of music functionality that you won't use when recording your podcast, and that functionality can get in the way. Next, you can't buy GarageBand by itself; it's part of Apple's iLife package, which includes several other applications you might or might not want.

tip

LAME originally stood for Lame Ain't an MP3 Encoder because it was an interface for existing ISO sample code that encoded MP3 files. Now, it does the encoding itself, and is supported by the LAME Project. You can see their work at www.lame.sourceforge.net.

Industrial Audio Software has an application designed strictly for podcast recording. iPodcast Creator has an interface that looks a great deal like the console at a radio station, so if you think of making a podcast as a recorded radio show, this will be very natural for you. iPodcast Creator does more than simply record your audio, though—it includes editing, ID3 tagging, XML creation, and FTP services, so there's more to learn in the package, but only one package to learn.

Windows Recording Software

Windows users have more choices when it comes to recording software than do their friends with Macs. There are many options for recording using either free or commercial software, beginning with Audacity, which provides recording and basic editing functions for Windows-based computers just as it does for Macs. You can also use Winpodcast, one of the earliest podcast-specific applications, created by Sascha Siekmann. Winpodcast is not just a recording application, since it helps with show notes, editing, tag creation, and other podcasting tasks.

Commercial software for Windows podcast creation is varied, but there are a couple of packages that provide audio recording as part of a larger suite of podcast-ready functions. MixMeister's Propaganda is a complete package for creating a podcast, with audio recording, editing, ID3 tag creation, RSS feed, and FTP functions in a package that moves through the process in a fairly straight line. Industrial Audio Software has a version of iPodcast Creator for Windows, along with iPodcast

Producer, which is designed with a more commercial customer in mind. The two companies take differing approaches to podcast creation, with Mixmeister taking a DJ/editing approach while Industrial Audio Software looks much more like a radio station's console.

Linux Recording Software

If you're looking for sheer numbers, it's hard to beat the variety of recording software available for Linux. It is also hard to imagine a wider range in capabilities and quality for software than can be found for Linux.

tip

New software for creating or working on portions of a podcast appear almost weekly. To get the latest list of products available for your platform, look at the tools section of www. ultimatepodcasting.com.

Much of the software available for Linux came into being because someone needed a single task accomplished and was willing to write some code to make it happen. This means that Linux software is much more likely than software for either Windows or Macintosh to do one thing, rather than have individual functions integrated into an operational suite. A good example of this is Audio Record Expert, a shareware program that records from sound card or line-in sources. This doesn't mean that there are no programs available that do more multiple jobs. Audacity, for example, does the same blend of recording/editing/ mixing tasks on Linux that it performs on the other major platforms. Other packages, such as MultiTrack, SLAB, SMIX, KMIX, and MixViews have strengths in various areas such as editing or mixing, though they perform multiple jobs with interfaces that run the gamut from command-line to gnome, KDE, and more.

tip

Most open-source Linux projects have a presence at Source Forge, found at www.sourceforge.net. While SourceForge is a must for Linux users, Macintosh and Windows users who are looking for software that goes beyond the usual suspects will find plenty to work with on the site, as well. Just be aware that there are enormous variations in the stability, maturity, and usability between different projects; be sure to carefully read the notes that accompany the downloads to understand what you're getting into before you install a package on your computer.

Audio Editing Software

As we've just mentioned, it's quite possible to find Linux software that specializes in editing, though even on the Linux side of things the majority of software products combine two or more major functions in a single package. Packages such as SMIX and KMIX focus on the editing side, and there is a piece of software, EasyPodcast, that performs all of the major functions required for creating a podcast, just like packages such as Propaganda and iPodcast Creator for Windows and Macintosh.

For any of the editing functions that you work with, one of the key issues to keep in mind is the file format that will be used in the editing process. Podcasts are almost always files in the MP3 format. Many editing packages don't work with MP3 files during the edit process, operating on WAV files (for example) until the final mix is reached. Once the sound file has been edited into its final form, it will need to be saved as an MP3 file, and decisions can be made about the quality of the MP3 file and the resulting size of the file.

The software you choose may have the ability to let you decide from a list of MP3 encoding speeds, usually expressed in kilobits per second, and ranging from 4 to 128 or more. You might want to try saving the same clip at different encoding speeds to see the difference it makes in both file size and sound quality. You'll see that it does make quite a difference when you go from 4 kbps to 96, and somewhat less of a difference when you go from 96 to 128. We've found that 96kbps is a good compromise rate between file size and quality, creating a file that is in the neighborhood of 10 Megabytes for a show that's around 20 minutes long, while maintaining a quality that is fine for someone listening over standard headsets or ear buds. Now, if you want to see why the MP3 file standard is so important for podcasting, compare the size of the WAV file you've been using in editing to the MP3 file that you'll publish as your podcast. The 10 Megabyte MP3 file came out of the 100+ Megabyte WAV file on your computer. I think we can agree that the MP3 is far better when you're going to be moving files around and storing them on a portable MP3 player.

If file size is becoming critical, and your podcast is spoken voice rather than music, you might also look at recording your file in monaural rather than stereo sound. When someone listens, your voice will be centered in the sound field, where most stereo recordings place a single spoken voice, so the difference will be unnoticeable by most folks—until they realize that the file transferred in about half the normal time. This is a great trick when you're doing a podcast of commentary or an interview.

FTP Software

The FTP system is built in to Windows, Macintosh, and Linux operating systems, so in one sense you don't need any additional software to transfer your podcast files from your desktop or laptop computer to the server. The amazing thing, though, is that there are so many different ways to accomplish a task that is a basic feature of virtually every operating system.

The first and most basic way of using FTP, and the way chosen by most truly hardcore computer experts, is the command-line interface, or CLI. The CLI is fast and elegant under the fingers of an expert, but it requires you to know the details of both client and server, the commands to link them together, and a high comfort level with entering commands through this most basic of user interfaces.

Next, a close tie to the operating system means that FTP can be accessed through many common applications. Popular web browsers, including Microsoft's Internet Explorer, can serve as the basic interface for FTP sessions. In Internet Explorer, you simply check the box in the Advanced options menu of the Options menu for the Enable Folder View for FTP Sites option. Now, you can drag and drop files from your desktop or My Computer folders into the folder that's in the browser window, and the two computers will handle all the details.

Using a browser method can work very well if the server you're transferring the podcast to provides access to anonymous FTP (that is, FTP with no user authentication or security), and you are only moving one file at a time. If you have a secure FTP site, or need to move a lot of files in one session (if, for instance, you're setting up a website for the first time), then you might want to look at an FTP client—software that's dedicated to nothing but sending files back and forth over an FTP connection.

Whether you are using the Macintosh, a Windows computer, or a Linux system, there are literally dozens of FTP clients available as freeware, shareware, or commercial software. Virtually all work in essentially the same way; you create a script that handles the address and login script (usually just your user name and password) for the server you're transferring to, then navigate to the correct subdirectory on both client and server. You'll see the files on the client on one side of the screen, with the server's files on the other. Now, you simply drag and drop or highlight and click on an arrow to show the direction of the transfer. There will likely be one more small detail you'll need to cover; the client will probably ask you whether the transfer is ASCII or binary. Here's your answer: Your podcast, photos, and any other file that aren't just plain text will be sent binary. The ASCII transfer is reserved for HTML, simple text (not word-processing files), and nothing else. When in doubt, use binary. When the transfer has finished, be sure to click the button for disconnect, and your podcast is ready to meet its listeners.

Budgeting for Bandwidth

Before you can sit back and wait for your listeners to tell you how much they love the podcast, you should be ready for one tiny detail. Many blogs and podcasting websites contain some language about how they'll handle "excess" bandwidth demand. Your first job is to figure out how many downloads constitute "excessive" and how to make sure your downloads each month total less than that.

Take a look at your podcast files. If you're like most people, you find that your average podcasts are all about the same size. For the sake of a good illustration and easy math, let's say that the average is 10 Megabytes. This means that 10 downloads will be 100 Megabytes of bandwidth, while 100 downloads is one gigabyte. If you actually had 100 downloads of your 10 Megabyte podcast, the total bandwidth would be a bit more than a gigabyte—the web page, pictures, and other information on your site all take up bandwidth, too.

Now that you know how to figure out the bandwidth, begin looking at your expected traffic levels, and how you'll deal with "the horror of success". You can either pay your service provider for more bandwidth, or you can unplug your server when you hit the monthly limit. If you want a successful podcast, you'll choose the former, with a Tip Jar, perhaps, to help offset the cost of bandwidth.

That's the basic list of hardware and software you need to get started on the road to podcasting. Now, let's start looking at the question of how you should be using all that nifty hardware and software.

The Absolute Minimum

Once you decide on your basic computing platform, it will be time to collect the hardware and software required for a podcasting studio.

Your podcast starts with the microphone, and a low-cost condenser mic will get you started. As you develop your podcast you can invest in a superior microphone.

Headphones are crucial for a successful podcast; they let you know how your listeners will hear the podcast.

You may decide to take your podcast production on the road. There are a variety of portable recorders, available for field recording.

There are many software options available for creating your podcast. You'll want to find options for recording, editing, FTP, tag creation, and uploading. There are a number of capable programs available that combine all the critical features for developing and managing podcast sites.

Every time someone downloads your podcast, it adds to your monthly download total. Keep an eye on the size of your podcast, since your user agreement with the ISP or blog-hosting site might include a limit on how much bandwidth is included in your monthly fee. Be proactive talking with your ISP about changing programs, even for a short time, to a plan with a higher bandwidth limit.

7

RECORDING YOUR PODCAST

It's time to put all the tools to use and record your first podcast! Knowing the right techniques for the studio will make your dialogue sound great. Then, you can add other voices to your podcast through professional-sounding interviews. When the studio is no longer big enough to hold your ideas, take your podcast into the field to bring "the real world" to your listeners! This chapter brings you the tips, techniques, and tools to make the quality of the recording match the quality of your content.

It's Showtime!

You've planned the perfect podcast, following the guidelines for show prep we covered in Chapter 6. As a result, you have the confidence of knowing just what you want to do and how you want to do it. Now it's time to get yourself into a frame of mind that will allow you to create a terrific show, not just this time but every time you get ready to hit the "record" button. To do that, a good place to start might be spending a few moments studying Serena Williams. No, Serena isn't doing a podcast—at least she hasn't started one yet! But what she does when she steps on to a tennis court contains an important lesson that can help your podcast tremendously.

Every time Serena gets ready to serve, she follows the same routine. She bounces the ball the exactly the same way every time. She readies her racquet the same way. She tosses the ball in the air the same way. And, finally, she takes the same swing—every time. Her routine before every serve doesn't vary from one serve to the next. She's able to focus because she has eliminated all the variables and all the distractions.

This same principle can work for you, too. You'll be able to consistently do your best work if you're able to develop a routine that eliminates as many variables in the studio as possible and allows you to focus, instead, on projecting your podcasting persona.

Some elements that your pre-podcast routine might include are

- Putting all of your show notes and any other materials you might need somewhere you can access them easily and quickly
- Going through your checklist one more time to make sure the settings on all your recording equipment and software are correct
- Making sure that the ringers on any nearby phones are turned off
- Checking to see that the batteries of any battery-powered equipment you're using are fresh

Developing a pre-show routine like this serves two important purposes. First, it lessens the likelihood of anything going wrong during your podcast. Second—and perhaps even more important—it works in an almost Pavlovian way to get your mindset and energy level ready for your show.

Recording Tips and Techniques

Here is a cafeteria selection of ideas that can make your recording sessions more consistent and more effective. Not every one of these will work for every podcaster, but some experimentation will help you uncover several that will work for you.

- Try standing while you record or, even better, try walking around.

  There's no rule that says you need to be stuck in a chair while you're recording. In fact, many podcasters find that it's easier to keep their energy level up during a podcast if they are standing or walking around. If walking around works for you, you should consider using a wireless headset. The important thing to remember is that your microphone, whether it's in your hand or attached to a headset, will pick up the vibrations from movements and brushing against clothing, your skin, or other things; this comes through on your podcast as thumps and scrapes. If you want to move around, record a practice session or two to make sure that you're not inadvertently putting lots of thumping and bumping sound effects into your podcast.

- Get used to keeping your eye on your levels.

Your recording equipment and/or software provides visual cues about whether or not you're recording at the proper level. Get in the habit of scanning these indicators, such as those shown in Figure 7.1, regularly. You'll have to force yourself at first but eventually it will become as unconscious as looking at your mirrors while you're driving. This will make it less likely that you'll wind up with an unpleasant surprise when you listen to what you've recorded.

The precise look of the level meters will vary from recording program to program, but all have a scale that starts with negative numbers around –32, goes up to 0, and then above zero to +6 or +12. The number to keep in mind is 0, because that's the point at which your recording will be at the maximum volume without danger of distortion. You'll want to keep your recording level as close to zero as much of the time as possible, and above zero as seldom as possible. In general, if you're recording and the needle or stack of bars on your meter never reach zero, then your recording is going to be softer than it should be, and your listeners will have to turn up the volume on their MP3 player to compensate. If the meter is showing a recording level that's at the top of the scale all the time then the odds are good that your sound will be distorted, "rough," and hard to understand much of the time.

Of the two problems, a low level is more readily fixable in the editing process—you can boost the level of the track as you're creating the final version (and we'll show you how to do that in Chapter 8, "Processing and Posting Your Podcast"). Distorted sound from a recording that was too "hot" is pretty much impossible to fix—you just have to go back and do it again.

- Maintain a mental picture of specific listeners while you're recording.

In Chapter 4, "Strategies for Planning Each Show," we discussed the importance of knowing your audience. Many podcasters find it helpful to take that concept a step further and develop a mental image of some specific listeners, then talk to those people when they record. In one way or another, every successful podcast is able to create a connection with its listeners. This technique can help make your communication sound more personal and less antiseptic.

FIGURE 7.1

Levels on your meters should stay below the "0" mark—going above that point means distortion: For a podcast that just sounds bad.

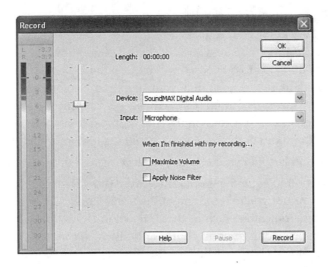

- If you're going to edit in post-production, pause for a moment after a stumble.

This technique isn't useful if you're going for a "live" feel to your show. If you're going to edit your podcast, however, you'll make your job a great deal easier if you pause for a moment of silence after a mistake you know you'll want to edit out. A pause will create a visual cue for you when you edit the sound file, making it easier to find the parts that need to be trimmed.

It's best if you've decided before you begin your recording whether you're going to edit the files in what's called "post-production" or just convert your recording to MP3 and post it on the Web. If you're going to edit your recording then plan to put a moment of silence before and after major topics, at the beginning and end of the session, and after any error, especially if you correct the error and then keep going. All of these pauses can easily be cut out during editing, and allow you more "elbow room" when it comes time to add sound, splice different sections together, or add sound effects and music to the final version.

- Record some "room tone."

In post-production, you will sometimes want to add some "silence" into your unedited recording. "Silence" is something of a misnomer, though. As you're recording your podcast, even when you're not speaking, the background of the environment in which you're recording contributes ambient noise to your recording. That ambient noise is known as "room tone." When you need to add a few seconds in which no one is speaking into your recording, if you added real silence it would stand out starkly from the rest of the track. Room tone, on the other hand, will blend right in.

The ambient noise in your room can vary considerably from one day to the next. Be on the safe side and record 10 seconds of ambient noise before each podcast and you'll never find yourself in a bind.

Interviewing Guests on Your Podcast

Interviews are a staple of the podcasting medium. They provide an opportunity for you to bring your listeners information and entertainment that you might not be able to deliver on your own. Like other aspects of audio communication, interviewing is a skill that you can develop and improve over time.

Here are some tips and techniques that will make your interviews livelier, more informative, and more engaging for your listeners:

- Do your homework.

  As a rule, interview subjects respond well to interviewers who demonstrate an interest in the topic at hand by having done some research before the actual interview. It's always a good omen for the rest of your interview when your guest asks, "How did you find that out?" Don't be afraid to keep a list of questions or facts in front of you while you're talking to your guests. Knowing that you won't forget something interesting can help keep you more relaxed in the discussion.

- Avoid the obvious.

  Unless there's a compelling reason to do so, it's usually not a good idea to put your guest in the position of repeating some story they've already told a dozen times or more. Most guests react by going into auto-pilot mode, which rarely makes for a riveting podcast. If there is groundwork that needs to be covered for your listeners' benefit, it is often better for you to do it as part of the preface to the interview itself.

- Make your questions as conversational as possible.

  This is particularly important when you're interviewing a guest who isn't accustomed to being interviewed. If you ask questions that sound like Raymond Burr in an old Perry Mason show, it can make your guest uncomfortable and, not surprisingly, make them feel as though they're being cross-examined. A conversational tone will make it easier for your guest to be conversational in return. As a result, they're likely to be more forthcoming.

- Listen carefully to what your guest is saying.

  Sure, you've got a lot to think about, keeping one eye on your recording equipment and the other eye on the time. Still, your most interesting interviews will involve a genuine interaction between you and your guest. That can only happen if you're paying close attention to what's being said and reacting to it rather than worrying about asking your next question. When your guest says, "Well, we've been doing this for three years now," the most effective follow-up question is *not*, "So, how long have you been doing this?"

TAKE A MOMENT TO EXPLICITLY GET PERMISSION TO PODCAST YOUR INTERVIEWS

It is distinctly uncool to record someone without his or her knowledge and explicit permission. In some instances, it may even be criminal. To protect yourself and make sure you're doing the right thing relative to your interview subject, take a moment after you've pressed the record button but before the interview has started to say something like, "I just want to make sure we're clear about the fact that I'll be using all or part of this interview in my podcast." You can edit that disclaimer out of the finished podcast file, but you'll have the raw file in your archives just in case any questions arise at a later date.

How Long Should You Keep Your Files?

One of the questions reporters deal with is, "How long should I keep my recordings and my notes?" In a perfect world, the answer would be to keep them as long as you might find them interesting, but in a world with libel, slander, and intellectual property laws, your considerations should go somewhat deeper than that.

Understand that the files we're talking about here are the raw audio files, photographs, and notes that you use to build your podcast. The podcast files themselves will, we suppose, be around as archives for as long as your feed is alive. For the source files, you have three broad options when it comes to a strategy: You can delete them immediately after you've completed the edit for the podcast, you can keep them forever, or you can decide on a length of time to keep them. The point is that you have a policy and stick with it while you're podcasting—we'll get into more depth on the reason in the next paragraph or two.

Deleting or discarding all your raw files adds a certain immediacy to everything you do (and an urgency to getting it right), but will keep you from going back and reusing material for later podcasts. Of the three options, this one is the most restrictive to your creativity—it's really "working without a net" when it comes to building a collection of podcasts. Keeping your files for a set length of time

> **tip**
>
> Take the time to label each of the CD-ROMs on which you store your raw materials. It's a good idea to write down the range of dates from the last backup until this disk was created. If you've decided to keep files for specific length of time, go ahead and put the "Discard on…" date on the label, too—it makes things easier when it's time for the trash bin.

balances the desire to revisit material with the reality of limited space in most buildings.

Of course, CD-ROMs really don't take up all that much space compared to the amount of data they'll store, so keeping stuff forever is an option. The key to this one is that, if you decide to keep things forever, you really take steps to do that; buy a banker's box and store your material in some sort of order just in case you need to get it out later.

The reason consistency is important is that someday, for reasons you can't now imagine, an attorney could come asking for those files. If you discard everything as soon as you're created the final product, you state that, prove that, and life goes on. If you keep everything forever, you provide the material. The problem arises if you keep most things forever, but for some reason didn't keep the piece of information they're looking for. Then, you get into tedious explanations and your life becomes more complicated than it should. Since we like simpler lives, it makes sense to just create a policy and stick to it.

ARCHIVE YOUR INTERVIEW FILES

There are several reasons you should consider archiving the raw files from your interviews. The most important is that you might need them to establish the accuracy of any quotes you might use from the interview in written form, such as a blog or magazine article. Another reason is to establish the context of any excerpts you might use from the interview. Finally, as we noted elsewhere, there are occasionally questions about the permission you received to use the interview. Your archival copy of the raw interview will allow you to address all of these issues definitively.

The cost of computer storage today is so low as to be almost nonexistent. In fact, a pack of 25 blank DVD-R discs costs less than $10 at your local office supply store. With storage so cheap, there's simply no good reason to not archive your interview files.

Recording in the Field

One of the great things about podcasts is that they can carry programs created anywhere. With some simple tools and basic techniques, you can record a podcast as easily in the park or the local coffeehouse as in your studio. With a headset microphone plugged into your laptop computer's sound card, the world is your studio! We have recorded simple podcasts in airports, on airplanes, in conferences rooms, and on the back porch. The real fun, though, comes when you want to take advantage of your remote location's unique qualities, rather than merely creating a standard podcast from a non-standard location.

When you get out of the studio, you really begin to take your listeners to places they couldn't go without your help. Rather than simply telling them about a street festival, you can let them walk along with you, hearing the sounds of the crowds and vendors and talking to the artists and neighborhood leaders who put the festival together. Instead of reading the names of the winners at the Friday night dirt-track races, you can take them into the stands to hear the roar of the engines and the thump of dirt clods landing around you—and you can ask people in the stands who they're rooting for and why they come to the races every week.

Moving your podcast into the field changes the basic dynamic of the recording and the experience you create for your listeners. While great content is still the most critical ingredient in a successful podcast, the right tools and techniques are the equivalent of a writer's well chosen words—they can make the experience dramatically more vibrant, immediate, and real for those listening to the podcast.

Your headset mic and laptop soundcard can allow you to record a vocal track in spite of a remote location. Working with remote locations can require a different approach to recording, and a different set of tools. In many remote sites, for example, a laptop computer is too large and unwieldy to make a useful recorder. If you'll be standing or walking around with your recorder in your hands, for instance, a laptop computer is almost impossible. In the same way, if going "on location" involves talking with other people for your podcast, the headset microphone loses in efficiency far more than it gains in enforced intimacy.

Working with Ambient Noise

Sound-seeing is taking the listener to a particular place at a specific time, allowing them to hear the sounds of a situation as though they were walking alongside you. Sound-seeing is all about making the most of the ambient sound, highlighting the aural landscape of a location to make the place seem real and immediate to your listener. In most cases, an omnidirectional microphone is the best option because it "hears" sounds from nearly every direction, just as your ears do when you're walking through a location.

The difficulty can come when you're trying to narrate the ambient sounds as you present them. If you want to narrate as you're walking through the scene, you'll need to make sure that the microphone is close enough to you, and oriented properly, to ensure that the narration is louder than the ambient sounds and distinct enough to be easily understood by the listener.

> **tip**
>
> Recording your narration of the sound-seeing podcast in your studio gives you time to listen to the ambient sounds and plan what you will tell your listeners. It's easy to record the narration in pieces that refer to the photograph you post, the sound recording you've made, or links to other websites.

Since it can be difficult to walk around, narrate a podcast, watch relative levels, and monitor a recording all at the same time, you will probably want to record your narration after you've recorded the sound-seeing ambient tracks. This gives you the opportunity to think about what you've heard and record a great narration in your studio. You then get to edit the tracks together, using a program such as Audacity or Propaganda, adjusting the relative levels of the narration and ambient sounds for greatest impact and intelligibility.

Of course, sometimes you're recording in the field but you don't want to focus on the ambient sounds. It may be that you're trying to interview someone or focus on a particular sound, and you don't want to include every surrounding sound at the same level. In these situations, you'll want to think about using a cardioid mic (for close-in vocals), or a shotgun or parabolic mic (for focusing on particular long-distance sounds).

FIGURE 7.2

Sound-seeing podcasts can give your listeners a real sense of a place—it's an exciting programming option to experiment with.

Regardless of how you decide to handle the ambient sounds, they are the critical component that separates field recordings from studio recordings. In the studio, ambient sounds are reduced to non-existence, while they are the critical component in a field recording. Learn to listen in 360 degrees, focusing attention on the sounds around you, as part of your preparation to take your podcast recording into the field. The result will be a podcast that's more interesting to far more people.

THE ABSOLUTE MINIMUM

Successful recording comes from planning carefully and keeping your eye on a couple of things, then capturing your own fascinating, enthusiastic self. Do a little bit of planning—have at least a rough idea of the topics you want to cover before you hit the Record button. Keep an eye on the recording level so your voice is what people notice, rather than the distortion. Finally, keep your surroundings in mind, whether that means keeping your microphone from brushing against your shirt or understanding that the garbage truck rolling past on the street will probably drown out your voice. It seems like a lot to keep track of, but with just a little practice, you'll find yourself able to automatically get the technical parts right so you can pay attention to what matters most—your content.

- Plan the broad outlines of your podcast before you start recording
- Let yourself be natural while you record—if that means walking around then walk around
- Be aware of your recording levels so your sound is neither too soft nor distorted
- Interviewing others can add variety and interest to your podcast
- With the right equipment, a podcast can be made virtually anywhere
- If you pay attention to the sounds around you, you can help your audience "sound-see" the place where you record

8

PROCESSING AND POSTING YOUR PODCAST

Recording the elements of your podcast is only the first step toward putting it in the ears of listeners. You must still make decisions on mixing and editing your podcast, decisions that will shape its sound toward smooth and polished or spontaneous and informal. In this chapter, we'll look at the techniques for helping you make the podcast sound the way you want during the mixing and editing stages of production. Once you've got the final product sounding the way you want, it will be time to "package" the podcast by converting it from the native format your recording software uses into an MP3 file, and set the ID3 tags that let listeners know what they're listening to as they watch the screen of their MP3 players.

Finally, when the MP3 file is ready to go, it's time to upload it to the website that hosts your podcast. You'll most likely upload your file using FTP, a protocol that's easy to use, fast, and doesn't have the file size restrictions associated with most email services.

Editing Techniques

It's possible to create a podcast by plugging your microphone into the sound card of your computer, hitting "record" on your software, and talking until you're through. For most of us, though, you'll want to combine several different pieces of audio to create a total podcast. You might start with some music, add narration, include more music or an interview, then finish with a "good bye" and some final music. Putting all those pieces together is a process called *editing*, and it's one of the critical skills of podcasting. Let's look first at the basic process.

Many of the sound-editing packages available for personal computers use a similar interface, so while the screen shots we'll use to illustrate the process may not be identical to what you see on your computer, they should be close enough to let you follow along. Most of the examples that follow were created with Propaganda, a program from Mixmeister. Why Propaganda? There were two main reasons: First, Propaganda's interface is similar to that used by many other recording and editing programs, including the interface of Audacity, popular free software. Next, Propaganda's interface made it easy to see what was going on with the sound file—and therefore easier for you to learn how to create your own podcast.

Thinking in Tracks

Electronic editing begins with the concept of *tracks*. If you think of each recorded segment that you'll be using to build your podcast as a separate track, you're moving in the right direction. In Figure 8.1, you see a screen with two tracks. The upper track is a short piece of music used as an introduction, while the second track is an interview.

Now, we could just let the music end and start the interview, but that would almost certainly leave us with some silence and an abrupt change between the two segments. It will be better if we move the second track to begin playing before the music ends. You can see what this looks like in Figure 8.2.

Now there's not an abrupt change, but we're left with another problem; the music and the interview are playing at the same volume. This means that we can't hear the first words of the interview, instead getting a confused jumble of sound that might be interesting but isn't at all what we're looking for in our podcast. It's time to learn how to "fade " from one track to the next.

It's Time to Fade

The first step in the fade process is figuring out when we want the first track, in this case the music, to start getting softer. After listening to the track, we figure out the best place for the music to begin its fade, and we set an edit point by right-clicking on that spot to see a menu like the one in Figure 8.3.

FIGURE 8.1

Each sound clip is called a track in electronic editing.

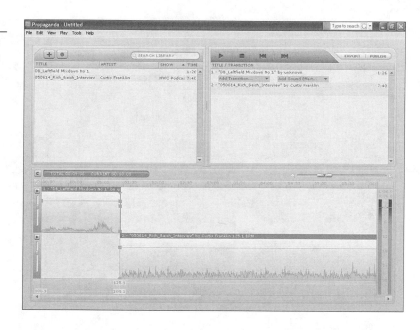

FIGURE 8.2

Overlapping the tracks is an important step in building your podcast.

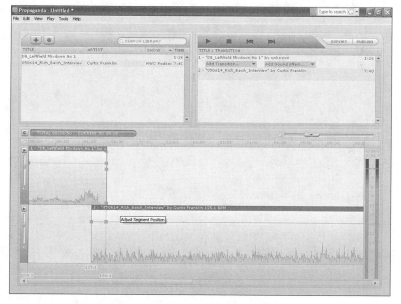

If we just varied the volume control at the single edit point we've just created, we'd end up with a track volume that consistently got quieter from the beginning of the piece until our edit point, then got louder again until the end of the track. You can see what we mean by looking at the volume line in Figure 8.4, where we've pulled the volume down at a single point.

FIGURE 8.3

Points are set that allow you to edit the tracks.

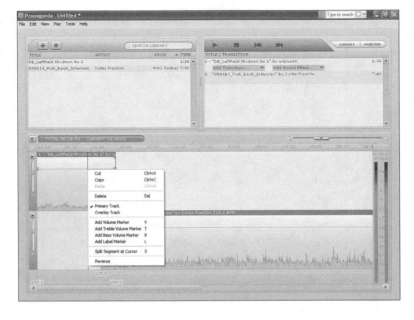

FIGURE 8.4

Changing the volume of a single point doesn't keep the volume at a consistent level.

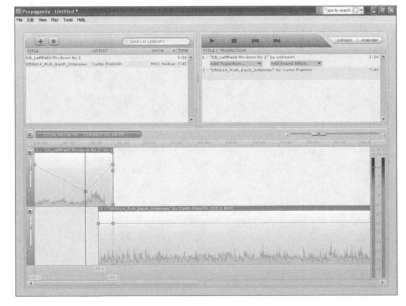

Since this isn't what we're looking for, we have to figure out how to keep the volume at one level until our initial edit point, then have it fade to another, lower volume level. The key to this is creating at least two more edit points, one at the end of the track, and another between the first edit point and the end of the track. The placement of this "in-between" edit point is important because it controls whether your fade is slow or fast. The closer the in-between point to the first edit point, the faster the fade will be; a point closer to the end will create a more gradual fade. In Figure 8.5, we've created our three edit points, and it's time to start adjusting the volume.

FIGURE 8.5

Using multiple points lets you set and hold a volume.

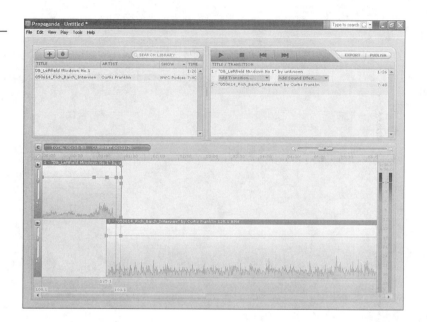

First, we'll create the fade by dragging the volume of the in-between edit point down to our desired level. Now, you can choose to take it all the way to silence, or you can merely make it very quiet and have the voice come in over the "background music" created by the fade. You'll probably want to try a particular level then listen to the result—in the beginning you'll almost certainly listen to several versions as you get a feel for the levels that work best for the sound you want your podcast to have. There's no right answer because every podcast sounds different, and the way you create your fades will contribute to the distinct sound of your podcast. In Figure 8.6, we've pulled the volume down to a point where the music is soft, but still audible as the speaking voices start.

We're not through, yet. While we've brought the sound level down, we have to keep it there. This is why we put the edit point at the end of the track, to help keep the sound level at the fade-out level we've decided is right. Since we didn't fade all the way to silence, we have a couple of options with our final end-point: We can either keep it at a consistent "background music" level set at the in-between point, or we can create a slow fade to silence. Now, you will obviously see that a fade can be created from two or three edit points if you want the sound level to steadily increase or decrease. If you want the rate of the fade to change during the fading process—something that we chose to do because it sounded better when we listened to it—you'll need to use more edit points. In Figure 8.7, we slowly fade out to silence as we move to the end of the clip.

FIGURE 8.6

Softer music "behind" the spoken track can be very effective.

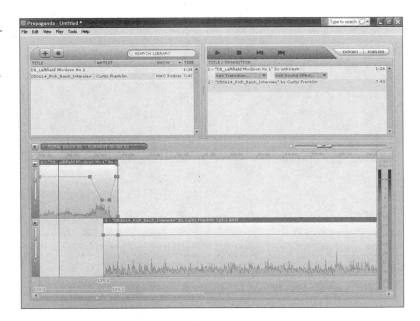

FIGURE 8.7

Gradually diminishing volume is called a fade.

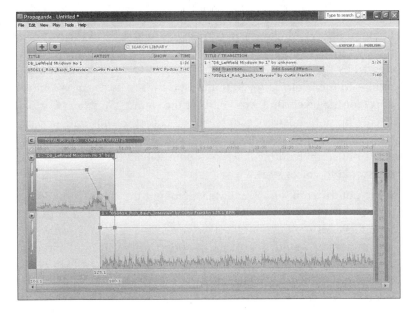

Building Blocks for a Podcast

So we've created our first fade, the most basic editing technique you'll be using in your podcast. Now, let's look at getting a bit more creative in adding pieces to our podcast.

Instead of just having a music intro and an interview, let's say we've decided that we want to record our own spoken introduction, or setup, to the interview. In our setup, we'll tell listeners who the interview is with, give them a little background information, and describe our reasons for wanting to talk with our interviewee in the first place. Just to keep things from getting dull, we'll add a little piece of music between the setup and the interview.

As long as we're on this kind of roll, we might as well record a concluding piece, or wrap up, for after the interview, to tell the listeners what it all means and why we're so happy to have been able to bring them this great interview. To keep things symmetrical, we'll want to have a little piece of music between the interview and the wrap up and then, of course, some music to ease our listener's transition from our podcast back to the real world. Wow, this is a pretty simple podcast, and we're up to seven separate tracks to edit together. Fortunately, each edit is as simple as the first we did, so let's take a look at our track layout in Figure 8.8.

FIGURE 8.8

A podcast can be built from many tracks.

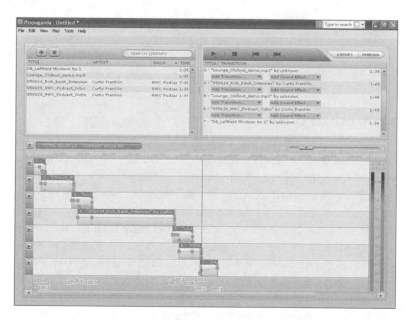

So we get the fades right, and everything is in the right order, but we notice a problem. In the interview, we introduce ourselves and our interviewee, and talk about where we are. That's fine, but now we're doing the same thing in our setup, so we've got some redundant information and it sounds kinda silly. We need to edit out the introductory stuff from the interview. Let's look at how we do that.

We start by once again setting edit points, just like we did for our fade outs. This time, we set one point at the very beginning of the track, and one at the point where we've just finished the introductions. If you look at the sound-wave image for the track shown in Figure 8.9, you can see that there's a distinct valley where we've stopped talking. When you watch the valleys, they can be a huge help in deciding where you need to put the edit points for cutting bits of a track.

FIGURE 8.9

Setting the point for a cut is just like setting the point for a fade.

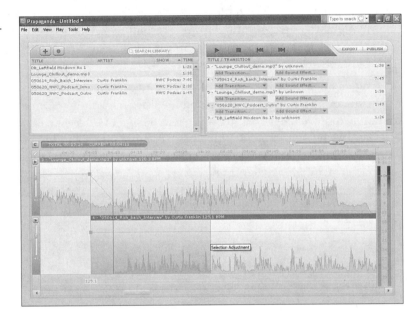

Decisions on Edit Points

Now, there is one thing you want to be careful about when you're deciding where to make cuts. First, if you're cutting out individual words or sounds, make sure that there's enough of a "gap" around the sounds you've selected so that the remaining words aren't jammed too close to one another, creating an unnatural sound. Listen to your cuts, and don't be afraid to use the "undo" command to restore the cut, and try again to get it right. Next, when you're making a cut that leads into a word or sound, make sure you cut in the valley. It can be tempting to really try to "tighten" a piece to save total run time, but you'll find that many times we make little sounds as we begin a word, and cutting the sound before the word can leave the voice sounding odd—once again, listen to the results, and don't be afraid to use undo to get back to a starting point to try the cut over if it doesn't sound the way you want. In Figure 8.10, we've made several changes; we've made our cut, copied the music so that it "loops" behind the interview, and the podcast is ready to go—well, except for some mixing we've decided we want to do before we let the podcast loose upon the world.

Mixing Techniques

Mixing is the process of making the sounds you've put together during the editing process sound good. You mix the individual tracks to make sure that your podcast listener isn't turning up the volume one moment, then yanking off her headset to avoid permanent hearing loss the next. You also mix to combine tracks—have two tracks playing at the same time—in order to make sure that the track you think is most important is the one that's most clearly heard.

Let's look back at the podcast we've been working to build. You know the music we used to lead into and out of our podcast? We've decided we like it, so we want to have it playing under our setup and wrap up tracks. The first thing we want to do is copy the music enough times to have it play under the complete setup. This process, called *looping*, is a common technique for creating a long-playing soundtrack behind speech or other sound. When we've done this, the track looks like the screen shown in Figure 8.10.

FIGURE 8.10

A short music track can be repeated many times to make a longer musical selection.

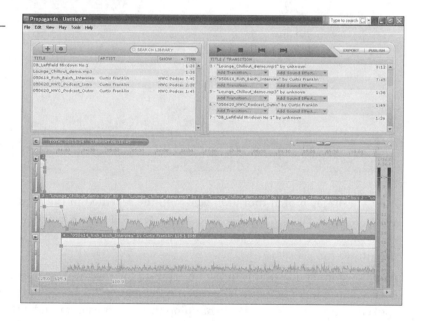

Extending Our Loops

There are two things we have to do now: First, we have to cut the last copy we made so that it matches the length of the setup. We'll use the technique learned earlier, setting edit points and cutting the last clip to length. Now, if we were going to be listening to this at a high volume, or trying to make it match a subsequent piece of music, then we would need to very carefully listen to the music and choose the right point in the beat pattern so that the cut made musical sense, just as we would be careful in editing spoken voices. In our case, though, the music will be in the background behind a spoken voice, and we'll do a fade to silence before the music leading to the interview starts.

The first step is to set the volume of the music so that it's behind the spoken setup. Since we already found a volume level we were happy with when we were creating the first fade, we just have to match it. We begin by setting a level low volume in the first clip, as we show in Figure 8.11.

FIGURE 8.11

Volume is set during the first repeat of the clip.

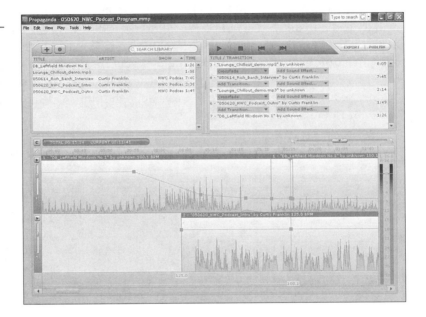

Now, we simply match that level across all the repeated music clips, as shown in Figure 8.12. Notice that we don't have to insert edit points in the repeated music clips, since we're not changing the volume during the clips, we're just resetting it for the entire clip.

Finally we insert edit points in the final music clip, because we do want a fade to silence. Since we're going to be matching the end of this music to the end of the spoken setup, and since we'll be bringing the next music up under these two tracks, we're not going to want just a simple straight-line fade, so we'll create several edit points and create the curved fade profile shown in Figure 8.13. How did we know how to create this profile? We listened. You'll do the same thing, listening to your tracks, creating edit points, and changing the volume to create the sound you want. Just remember that, whether you're using 2 edit points or 20, the process is the same. You don't have to get flustered or confused; just keep moving the volume at each edit point until your podcast sounds the way you want it to sound.

FIGURE 8.12
Once the level is set, it can be carried across all clips.

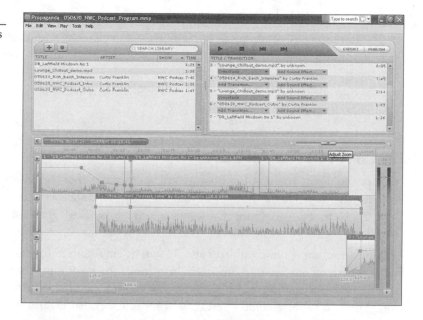

FIGURE 8.13
Listening will tell you how to shape the fades and crescendos.

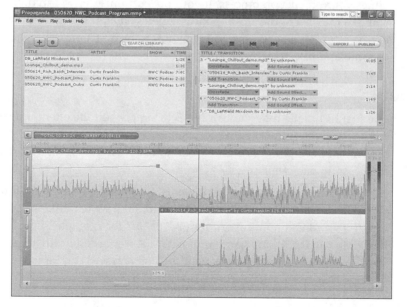

Building on the Cross-Fade

This process that we've just gone through, lowering the volume of one track while raising the volume of another, is called a "cross-fade," and it's one of the basic techniques used by DJs in creating dance mixes and long-format radio music programs. You can move the tracks back and forth on the timeline (which you see at the top of the track portion of every screen shot) to make sure that beats match, and that the music flows smoothly from piece to piece. How do you make sure that the music matches? You guessed it—listen. Watching the sound wave display can help, but differences between the way the display and your ears react to different sounds means that there's no real way to do it purely based on the display. You have to use your ears when you're mixing tracks.

To Clean or Not to Clean

One of the things you'll notice about your recordings is that they aren't perfect. Sometimes the problems are so bad that the only real option is to re-record a particular track, but more often there will just be some misplaced words, stray sounds, or odd background noises on the recording. The question is, what do you do about it?

The first decision is philosophical: Should you do anything to the file at all? There are podcasters who feel that one of the charms of the medium is that you hear dedicated amateurs creating audio programs, and that it's best to hear them "warts and all." This is a perfectly valid point of view for many podcasts, and it certainly simplifies your production process. If your podcast must answer to no one but you, and you like the idea of the "raw" podcast, then you can skip on to the next section. If, on the other hand, you need to know how to recover from sonic problems, let's look at some options.

Cut It Out

The first technique that you can use is to simply edit the offending sound out of the track. This is easiest if the sound is very short and louder than the other sound at that moment. Figure 8.14 shows a sound like this—the result of someone accidentally hitting a microphone.

Now, we listen to the track to hear what's going on behind the thump. If it's a vowel sound in the middle or at the end of a word, then we're probably OK just editing it out. If it's during a hard consonant ("K" or "T", for example), it's going to be much harder to clip the thump without making the word sound rather odd. In this case, we were lucky, and the edited track with the pop removed can be seen in Figure 8.15.

Filters for Clarity

If just editing the offending sound out isn't an option, there are a number of different filters and processors you can try. Your podcasting software may come with some built-in, and there are many available free or at very low cost on the Internet. Let's look at some of the possibilities:

FIGURE 8.14

A spike is a very brief, sharp sound.

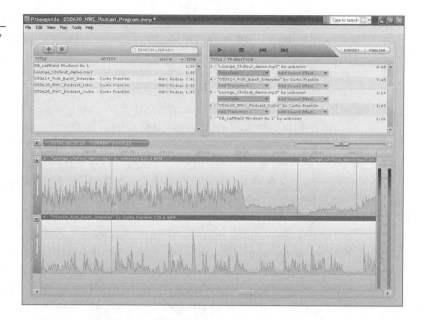

FIGURE 8.15

A short spike can often be removed without any effect on the surrounding program.

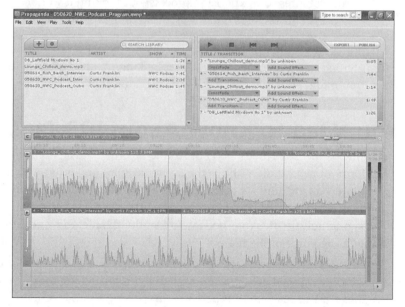

■ Equalizer—An equalizer breaks the sound spectrum up into separate bands, and allows you to control the volume of each band separately. If you have an annoying, constant noise that's at a specific pitch (from machinery, for example), you can use an equalizer to "notch" the particular frequency of the sound and eliminate the noise. This is most effective if the noise is not in one of the bands that is shared by the human voice.

■ Noise Filter—A noise filter takes advantage of the fact that the voice that you're recording tends to be the loudest thing on the track. Many noise filters work by eliminating any sound that doesn't reach a certain volume. This type of filter is commonly referred to as a noise gate. With these, when you're not talking, nothing is being recorded, though time will pass so that the flow of the recording sounds natural. These can be very effective at eliminating low background noises, but you should be aware that the "room noise" will be recorded when you're talking, but not when you're silent, leading to a very unusual sounding recording. There are times when it's the only way to get a usable track, but be sure to try it before using this filter for anything critical.

■ Compressor—Using a compression filter can reduce many sounds that lie just outside the volume and spectrum of the voice you're recording. This will also change the sound of the voice, though you might like the result. If you re-expand the recording in a subsequent step, much of the noise can be left behind, while the voices return to something closer to the original sound. Many of the voices in the commercial songs you hear have been through this compression/expansion process, but making it work can be a complex process that requires a lot of listening and experimentation.

No matter which filter or process you decide to try, there is absolutely no substitute for listening and experimentation. After looking at, and listening to, the possibilities, you might end up looking anew at the "raw" option, and that's just fine.

What You Need to Know About ID3 Tags

The MP3 standard is pretty good at storing recorded music information. In its original form, though, it didn't have the ability to store any information *about* the recording—no facilities for carrying title, artist, album, date, or any of the other facts we use to organize the recordings in our collection. Think about it—there was, in the original specification, no way to identify the file and its contents except through the name of the file.

Fortunately, there were, pretty quickly following the development of the spec, those who recognized the need for some system to organize files, and ID3 was born. In the original ID3V1 specification, there were fixed lengths and locations for the information, which was limited in scope and contents. These limitations were addressed in ID3V2, which became the version of ID3 tags used by most MP3 players and software. The only reason to think about ID3V1 is that there are still some users with software that can only read the older tags; if you want the maximum compatibility and can live with the limitations of the earlier version, you can specify ID3V1 when you're writing your final podcast file. It's possible, in fact, to use both, and many people do in order to cover the greatest number of users. Most ID3 tag editors clearly show which tags are used in a particular specification, and there are many fewer tags to worry about in ID3V1. For the rest of this section, we'll assume that you're going to use ID3V2 for your podcasts.

FILE 8.16

ID3 tags can be viewed with iTunes.

When you look at an MP3 player, the screen generally shows the name of the song, the album, and the artist, and may include additional information such as genre and the art from the album cover. You can often look at this same information in the software you use to link the MP3 player with a personal computer; Figure 8.16 shows a screen containing ID3 tags (or information) in Apple's iTunes software.

It's possible to use a product such as iTunes to edit the ID3 tags for your podcast before you upload it to your website. Most podcast recording software allows you to edit the tags when you're making the original recording or creating the edited file prior to upload. Figure 8.17 shows the menu for creating ID3 tags in iPodcast Producer. Notice that there are many fields that you can provide information for; in just a moment, we'll look at how you should fill those in. Before we do, though, let's look at one more option for providing ID3 information.

There are a number of shareware, open-source, GPL, and commercial products that are ID3 tag editors. With these editors, it is generally possible to edit many more of the parameters that exist in ID3V2 tags than are accessible through most recording, podcast production, or MP3-player synchronization programs. One such program is ID3-TagIT, a free software package developed by Michael Pluemper. The screenshots in Figure 8.18 were taken from ID3-Tagit as it manipulated the ID3 tags for the Science@NASA podcast. Note how rich the options are for including information in the ID3 tags—information that can be used for organizing, finding, and using your podcast.

FIGURE 8.17
Podcast creation
software allows
you to create
ID3 tags.

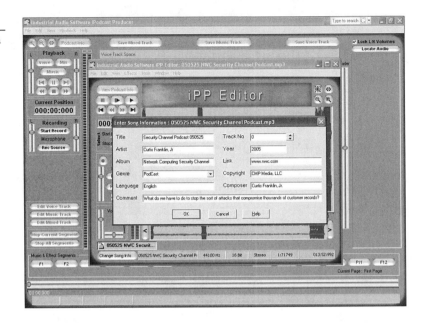

FIGURE 8.18a
ID3V2 allows
many tags to be
established.

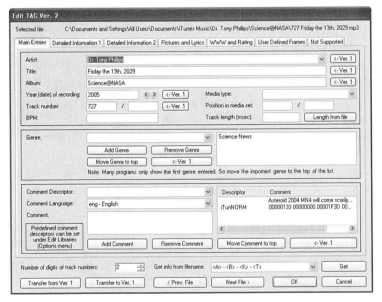

FIGURE 8.18b

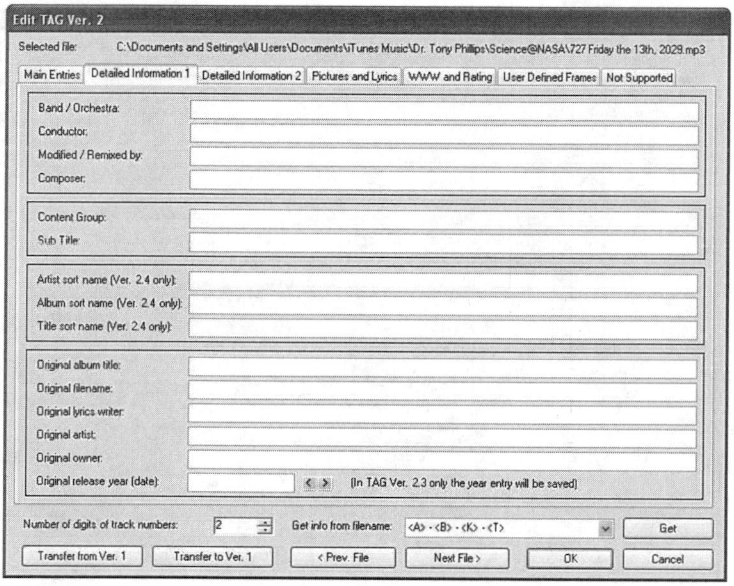

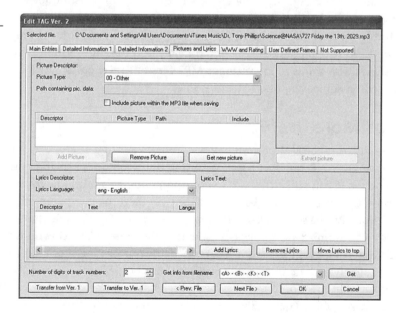

FIGURE 8.18c

FIGURE 8.18d

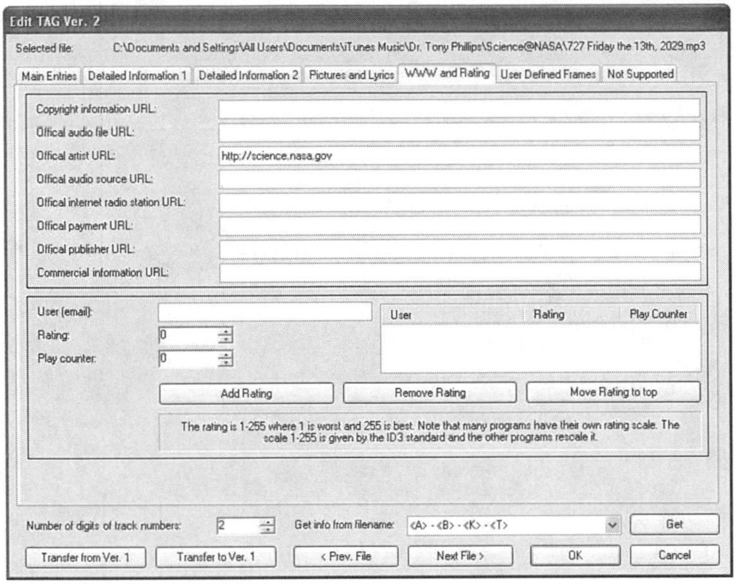

With the options for how to edit ID3 tags covered, the question moves to "What should the ID3 tags say?" Here is where things get interesting for you, and your podcast gets considerably more (or less) interesting for your listeners. First, know that we're fans of complete information in the ID3 tags. It takes only a moment or two to fully populate the critical tag fields, and the information is valuable to any listener who wants to organize his MP3 files or find a particular file (like yours) based on something besides your name.

Making Tags More Useful

The first and most important factor to make your tags useful to your listeners is to be consistent. Remember that the sorting and searching is being done by a computer, so if you make changes to your name (adding a middle initial sometimes, or using Liz instead of Elizabeth a time or two) then the computer will see two different authors. By the same token, changing the name of your podcast, or changing the way you number your podcasts, makes a huge difference. Do you want to sequentially number your podcast ("This is podcast number 14"), or refer to your podcast by date? It's a little thing, but consistent numbering makes it possible to see all the podcasts in order on an MP3-player playlist. The same is true of the "Album" field, which you should generally use to refer to your podcasts as a collection, with each individual podcast playing the role of a "track" on an album.

There are some conventions that have been picked up by podcasters that will make things easier for your listeners. Under "Artist," you should list your name only—your guests (if any) can go into a notes field. The "Album" name is the name of your podcast, which should not change from recording to recording. "Track

Number," on the other hand, should change each time, increasing by one with each new episode. You should also choose a genre, whether "spoken" or "podcast," that you keep consistent between recordings. Keeping these tags the same from one recording to another (with the exception of the "Track Number" tag) will help your listener organize podcasts and find the specific show she's looking for. She will appreciate this thoughtfulness on your part, tell her friends how wonderful you are, and generally help promote your podcast far and wide.

As you're naming your podcast, you can be quite creative, but remember that many MP3 players have a limited number of characters that can be displayed at one time. Some iPod models, for instance, can display 19 characters at a time. While the display will generally begin to scroll when an MP3 player's "cursor" is on a track title, the first few characters are what the user will see when scrolling through a playlist. You'll want to be careful how you choose the first dozen or so characters of your podcast's name to make it easy to find among hundreds of files on an MP3 player.

Once you've decided on a plan for ID3 tags and edited the tags on your completed podcast, it's time to upload it to a hosting site. In most cases, that will mean using software that understands FTP.

Using FTP

The File Transfer Protocol, or FTP, is one of the basic protocols used by Internet software. It allows large files to be moved around on the Internet without the necessity for the sort of excess baggage required by HTML or email protocols. The odds are good that you'll use FTP to move your podcast to the website—the only question is whether you have to know about FTP. Many of the services of the sort we'll talk about later in this chapter hide all the FTP details from the user.

If you do have to use a basic FTP program to send your files, you'll find that it's not complicated as long as you know a couple of things about the server to which you're sending. There are a number of shareware or free FTP clients (that's the software that sits on your computer) available, and all work in pretty much the same way. Figure 8.19 shows one of the clients available for Windows, FTP Commander. In this screen shot, we've connected to a basic FTP server, and you can see the files on our local computer on the left, the remote FTP server on the right, and arrows that command files to be moved from one to the other in the middle of the screen.

The first question to be answered is whether the site you'll be uploading to accepts "anonymous" FTP. That means it doesn't require any sort of user name or password from someone who wants to send a file. To reach a server that supports anonymous FTP, all you need to know is the address of the server, which will likely be ftp.something.com. Figure 8.20 shows the dialog box in which you set up the information to reach a new server. Notice that there's a check box for anonymous FTP—this is a very common way of doing things.

FIGURE 8.19

An FTP client helps move large files on the Internet.

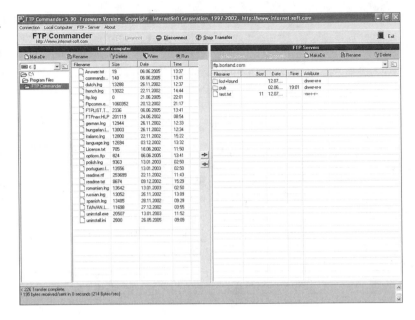

FIGURE 8.20

Anonymous login requires a simple check box in the client.

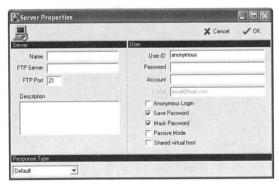

Because FTP is a service that is part of most operating systems, and the location for the files is not included in these basic services as it might be when FTP is part of an application or dedicated podcasting service, you may need to know which directory your file will go into when you place it on the server. You will generally get to the necessary directory on the server the same way you get to the right directory on your computer, with pointing and double-clicking. As you begin to work with FTP, there are only a few things that you might need to know in order to fill in the necessary boxes in a dialog box:

- The resource locator (address) of the FTP server
- The directory into which your files will go
- Whether your FTP server accepts anonymous file transfers

- If it doesn't take anonymous transfers, your user name and password
- The location of the files on your computer

Of course, choosing the right service to host or support your podcast can make knowledge of FTP services unnecessary, as they take care of all the gritty details and smooth your way to a published podcast.

Services That Will Make Your Podcasting Easier

While every aspect of posting, hosting, and syndicating your podcast can be handled on your own website (if you have one), you may decide that it's easier, cheaper, or more effective to use the services of companies that serve podcasters and/or bloggers.

Liberated Syndication (www.libsyn.com)

Some podcasters appreciate the technical aspects of putting a show together, getting it up on the Web, and getting it syndicated. For other podcasters, however, technology is a necessary evil, something they put up with to create and share their shows. If you're in this latter group, you might want to check out the site for one-stop podcasting services.

LibSyn charges a monthly fee ranging from $5.00 to $30.00, depending on how large your podcast files are and how often you post new shows. All you have to do is create your podcast, and LibSyn will do the rest. For your monthly fee, LibSyn will provide you with

- Storage for your podcasts
- A blog "engine" that allows you to post show notes
- RSS syndication for your podcast

For many podcasters, a big part of LibSyn's appeal is that it does not meter your bandwidth. As a result, when your podcast starts to become popular, you don't have to worry about getting hit with unexpected charges for the additional bandwidth.

Feedburner (www.feedburner.com)

Feedburner offers a variety of services for podcasters. As you might guess from the company's name, these services are centered around the creation and ongoing management of your RSS feed.

The mostvaluable of these services for serious podcasters is the generation of usage statistics, especially statistics about the overall listenership of your podcast. If your ultimate objective is to generate revenue with your podcast, the information that Feedburner generates will prove invaluable.

Feedburner also offers tools designed to ensure that your feed works with all the popular RSS feed readers and displays properly on RSS-enabled browsers.

Feedburner's basic service is free. Packages that provide more detailed usage statistics start at $4.99 per month (depending on the number of feeds you're tracking).

Podshow.com (www.podshow.com)

Podshow.com also offers a variety of services designed to simplify the posting, hosting, and syndication of your podcast. Package details were not available at press time.

Odeo (www.odeo.com)

Odeo also offers a variety of services designed to simplify the posting, hosting, and syndication of your podcast. Package details were not available at press time.

Hosting Companies

If you're very serious about your podcasting, you may decide that you want complete control over the distribution chain for your podcast—its feed, its hosting, and its ongoing management. If that's the case, you'll want to host your podcast and its RSS feed from your own website.

There are numerous hosting companies that can provide you with a home on the Web your podcast needs. You should know that the web hosting business is very competitive. With a little bit of shopping around, you're sure to find a web hosting package that provides a combination of support, capacity, and price that's right for you.

As you evaluate hosting companies, here are a few podcasting-specific matters you'll want to consider:

- How much storage do they offer? Your podcast files will be large, generally somewhere between 5 and 20 megabytes. With files of that size, your storage requirements are not trivial. How much server space does your host company provide?

- What do they charge for bandwidth? Bandwidth is the total number of bytes transferred off of your server in a given length of time. Most hosting plans define an allowable amount of bandwidth each month for a particular price. Bandwidth allowances and overage charges can vary dramatically from one hosting company to another. Since podcasting is a bandwidth-intensive undertaking, this is an important issue that you'll want to explore thoroughly before you make a decision. How much bandwidth are you allowed to use each month? What happens if you exceed that allowance?

■ Does the company support blogging software and PHP scripts? If you're going to host your podcast from your own website, you'll certainly want to host the accompanying shownotes blog from the same site. Some web hosts offer installation and support for the more popular open-source blogging packages such as WordPress. At a minimum, however, your web host must offer support for PHP scripting, the technology that underlies most blogging software.

One hosting company that offers an attractive package is PowWeb (www.powweb.com). PowWeb's one-size-fits-all offering is more than adequate for most podcasters. For less than $100 per year, it features WordPress installation and support as well as generous storage and bandwidth allowances.

THE ABSOLUTE MINIMUM

Once you've recorded your podcast, you're just a few simple steps from getting it ready for Internet distribution. The first set of steps involves editing the tracks together.

When editing your tracks, be sure to line them up so that a slight overlap eliminates total silence in the gaps between recorded pieces of the podcast. You can set edit points in the individual tracks to mark places where one track will begin getting quieter, so that the next track can come to the fore.

Once the basic tracks are edited together, you can begin mixing to achieve the best sound. Copying a short piece of music over and over, or looping, can provide a music background to long stretches of speech. When tracks meet, reducing the volume of one while raising the volume of the next can create a very smooth, professional-sounding transition. Individual tracks can be cut to make their length exactly match those of other clips. With length and volume established, you can decide on the question of cleaning the tracks.

Cleaning can eliminate stray noises, mistakes, or unwelcome sounds in a recording. Some podcasters clean all tracks; others like the "raw" sound with noises left in. Either can be correct—it's your choice.

After the podcast sounds the way you want it, it's time to add the ID3 tags that allow your listeners to sort, find, and organize your podcasts. Setting the tags is simple using an MP3 player, your podcast creation software, or a standalone ID3 editor. Remember that it's better to have complete tags, and that your tags should be consistent from program to program so that all your podcasts will be together when a listener's playlists are sorted. When you're creating the tags, think about the screens that display information on portable MP3 players; virtually all have limits on how

continues

many characters they can display, so brevity can be a virtue when it comes time to name your podcast or episode.

Most of the time, you'll use the Internet's File Transfer Protocol (FTP) to place your podcast on the server. If you have to set up the connection yourself, you'll find it easy if you look for the type of connection required (anonymous or authenticated), and think about where your files are going.

You might not have to think about FTP at all if you choose the right podcasting service. You owe it to yourself to check out the possibilities, so that you can concentrate on producing a great podcast, rather than supporting a website.

PART III

Distributing Your Podcast to Listeners

9

PUBLIC SYNDICATION

With your podcast files prepared and ready, it's time to let the world hear what you've created. You could simply put the file up on a web server and tell people to click on a link, but automated downloads and synchronizing with portable MP3 players are among the strengths of podcasting. You allow your listeners to take advantage of this automatic synchronizing by creating small files that implement RSS—Really Simple Syndication or, in another version, Rich Site Summary—on your site.

RSS, a special application of XML, allows readers who use one of the many RSS reader or podcast receiver software packages to click on a single link placed on your website, and then have their software check for new podcasts on a regular basis. When they find a new podcast file on your server, their computer will download it automatically, then place it on their MP3 player at the next synchronization session. Now, it's important to understand that RSS is used for many things that don't involve podcasts. News sites, blogs, weather alerts, product announcements, and many other pieces of information can be served through an RSS feed, and captured by a reader that won't handle podcasts at all. We're going to be talking about RSS and XML without paying much attention to these other uses, but you shouldn't forget that there are lots of other RSS and XML applications out there.

In this chapter, we'll look at what XML and RSS are and how you create an RSS document. We'll then talk about how you tie all the pieces of RSS and your podcast together, and how to be listed on all the big podcasting directories that can bring thousands of listeners to your podcast.

In the next chapter, we'll look at ways you can limit those who listen to your podcast, but for right now we'll assume that you're ready to release your podcast to the world—let's go.

An Overview of RSS

To understand RSS, you have to start with XML. XML stands for eXtensible Markup Language. In simplest terms, XML does for computers and software what HTML (Hypertext Markup Language) does for humans—it provides a common, standardized way to present information. When you look at an XML file, you'll see something that looks a lot like an HTML file, with tags, descriptions, and text. The two look alike because they're related, both derived from SGML, the Standard Generalized Markup Language that is the granddaddy of many current markup languages. What you're seeing, though, is a description of data and how it's arranged. XML is the language that more and more applications and control systems use to pass data between one another, but we're most interested for its use in one type of application: RSS readers.

Now, as you begin to think about building an RSS feed ("feed" is what the RSS and its related content is called), you should be aware that there are several versions of RSS floating around. There are several reasons for the multiple versions, but you don't need to worry about them. You just need to know of two versions, and stick to one of them for your podcast.

A Bit of History

The first versions of RSS were published by Netscape and further developed by Dave Winer at UserLand. The initial version was designated RSS 0.90, which was followed by 0.91, 0.92, 0.93, and 0.94. The latest version of this branch of RSS development is RSS 2.0. The only early version still in common use is RSS 0.91. It has the advantage of being very simple, but it is very limited in terms of the information the RSS feed itself can carry. Most people who like Winer's way of building RSS have now moved to RSS 2.0, which has a much richer set of metadata options (that is, many more options for including information about the podcast, blog, or article that the RSS feed points to), but is still less "verbose" than the other major RSS specification,

RSS 1.0. For a variety of reasons, most of the current crop of podcast aggregators (applications that find and download podcasts you've subscribed to) work with RSS 2.0—you can experiment with RSS 1.0, but for compatibility with the majority of podcast listeners, you'll want to write your RSS using the 2.0 (or 0.91) specifications.

> **tip**
>
> If you want to write the smallest and simplest RSS file possible, use RSS 0.91; you can easily move to RSS 2.0 if you find that you need to include more information about your podcast. If conforming to standards is important (say, because your company has that as a part of their development standards), then learn about RSS 1.0 as a possible future direction.

RSS and Beyond

While UserLand was still working on early versions of its RSS, a working group affiliated with the W3C developed an RSS version that is compliant with RDF, the Resource Description Framework that the W3C designed to standardize the way people use metatags. RSS 1.0 is based on a set of standards developed and maintained by an independent group, rather than an individual, and so will be more attractive to some users. It is, on the other hand, rather more verbose than RSS 2.0, and offers little difference in the type of information it can carry.

In the meantime, the folks at UserLand have developed yet another standard that is being used by a growing number of directories and aggregators. OPML (Outline Processor Markup Language) is a specialized offshoot of XML that describes RSS feeds in an outline form and makes exchange of feed and directory information possible in a standard way. Let's take a look at a podcast in RSS 0.92 and the feed described in OPML.

Let's take a look at the same podcast described in the two different standards.

Listing 9.1 A Sample Feed in RSS 0.92

```
<?xml version="1.0"?>
<rss version="0.92">
  <channel>
    <title>Absolute Beginner's Guide to Podcasting</title>
    <link>http://ABG2Podcasting.com/</link>
    <description>The Stuff You Need to Know</description>
    <item>
      <title>Second Beginner's Podcast</title>
      <link>http://ABG2Podcasting_2.mp3</link>
      <description>The Second Podcast</description>
    </item>
```

Listing 9.1   (continued)

```
    <item>
       <title>First Beginner's Podcast</title>
       <link>http://ABG2Podcasting_1.mp3</link>
    </item>
  </channel>
</rss>
```

In Listing 9.1, you can see a simple feed developed in RSS 0.92. There are many features available in this version of RSS that aren't used here, because this is designed to be a minimal feed—something that you could emulate to put a podcast in front of the public with minimal muss and fuss. Notice that there are a couple of lines at the top to tell the software reading the file what it's dealing with, then a brief description of the channel (that's the total collection of your podcasts) and the podcasts themselves.

LISTING 9.2   A Sample Feed in OPML

```
<opml version="1.0">
  -<head>
     <title>playlist.xml</title>
     <dateCreated>Mon, 01 Aug 2005 07:24:55 GMT</dateCreated>
     <dateModified>Fri, 5 Aug 2005 09:24:39 GMT</dateModified>
     <ownerName>Curtis Franklin, Jr.</ownerName>
     <ownerEmail>curt.franklin@gmail.com</ownerEmail>
     <expansionState>1,3,17</expansionState>
     <vertScrollState>1</vertScrollState>
     <windowTop>164</windowTop>
     <windowLeft>50</windowLeft>
     <windowBottom>672</windowBottom>
     <windowRight>455</windowRight>
  </head>
  -<body>
    -<outline text="Podcasts">
       <outline text="Absolute Beginner's Guid to Podcasting Podcasts. "/>
    </outline>
    -<outline text="July Podcasts">
       <outline text="First Beginner's Podcast" type="podcast"
       f="http://ABG2Podcasting_2.mp3"/>
       <outline text="Second Beginner's Podcast" type="podcast"
       f="http://ABG2Podcasting_2.mp3"/>
       <outline text="Third Beginner's Podcast" type="podcast"
       f="http://ABG2Podcasting_3.mp3"/>
```

```
      </outline>
    </body>
</opml>
```

When you look at a feed for the same podcast in OPML, you first see that there are additional lines at the top of the file to describe information about the entire podcast collection and how certain elements are to be displayed. If you look more closely, you'll see that there are outlined items, and space to collect an entire group of items (or groups of groups) within the body of the document. Remember, as with so many other pieces of technology, OPML wasn't designed specifically for podcasting, but it has found growing use for this new purpose. More and more aggregators are accepting OPML, as are most of the podcast directories. Learning both RSS 0.92/2.0 and OPML will maximize your ability to connect your podcast with individual aggregators and directory listings.

There are a handful of things you need to keep in mind as you're building your RSS code. First, aim for a balance in the information you put into the various elements of the file. Titles, for example, should be just long enough to be unique. If you give your podcasts cryptic names in the title blocks of your RSS, it's quite possible that a confusing, cryptic name will be what your listeners see when they download the file. Using file descriptions that are too long, on the other hand, can crowd the screen when a potential listener looks at the information. Balance is key.

You should also be careful not to include special characters or formatting in the fields of your RSS feed. They will display inconsistently in the various RSS and podcast clients, and could cause formatting problems in the way information is shown.

Finally, you should be sure to use the elements provided in the specifications to move information into the RSS feed. RSS 2.0 allows for most types of information to be included in the feed; if you need to include more than the basic information then look at the specifications to be sure you're putting it in the right place.

After you have created your RSS feed, you can check it for validity and correctness by using one of the available online validators. Among the validators you can use to check your RSS feed are

> ■ Feed Validator
>   http://feedvalidator.org/
>
> ■ Walidator.com
>   http://www.walidator.com/

tip

More information about, and the specifications for, the RSS standards can be found online. For RSS 1.0 information, go to http://purl.org/rss/1.0/. For RSS 2.0 information, go to http://rss.userland.com/. For OPML, go to http://www.opml.org.

- CZWeb.org

  http://validator.czweb.org/userland-rss.php

- Redland Validator

  http://librdf.org/rss/

- Allpodcasts.com

  http://www.allpodcasts.com/Tools/RSSValidator.aspx

Remember that the validators will tell you whether or not the code you've written is correct from an XML and RSS point of view—whether your code complies with the standards and meets the rules of the language. They won't tell you whether your feed will work—that has to come from the combination of validation and testing.

Of course, if you would like to have a piece of software generate the RSS feed for you, several options are available. These programs will scan the pages you've written, including any podcasts, photos, or other materials, and generate the RSS to allow your readers or listeners to subscribe to the feed. Among the RSS feed generators available are

- Podcastamatic

  http://bradley.chicago.il.us/projects/podcastamatic/

- Podcast RSS Feed Generator

  http://www.tdscripts.com/webmaster_utilities/podcast-generator.php

- DirCaster

  http://www.shadydentist.com/
  wordpress/software/dircaster

This list is far from exhaustive, since it's not terribly difficult to build an RSS generator and new ones are being released each month. You should look at two or three, try them with the code for your page, and see what sort of RSS code they deliver. Always remember to run the RSS generated by one of these programs through a validator before you place it on your site—programs can write code that's just as bad as anything a human can create.

You can also generate good RSS code with the automatic features of many blog hosts used

> **tip**
>
> If you want to have your podcast listed in Apple's iTunes podcast directory, you'll need to learn some new RSS tags. Most are similar to the RSS code you'll write for your usual podcast feed with slight differences. For a complete list of the tags and techniques you'll need, go to http://phobos.apple.com/static/iTunesRSS.html.

by podcasters. Blogger (www.blogger.com), Radio Userland (radio.userland.com), and WordPress (www.wordpress.org) are just three of the hosting services or server applications that can help build the RSS code for you when you use them to host a blog.

The final step in having the RSS feed on your site is to have a graphical "button" that visitors can click on to have their iPodder or other software read the RSS file. There are two widely used buttons—one labeled "XML", the other labeled "RSS"—which you upload to your site (each is a small .GIF-format image), then display on your page with your RSS feed as the target when the user wants to copy the RSS to paste into their podcast aggregator. It's simple, and has become the standard way of displaying the fact that you have an RSS feed on your site.

Enclosure Tags

In the beginning (RSS 0.92), RSS carried attached files (such as MP3 files) to RSS readers through a mechanism called *enclosure tags*. While most podcast listeners will use one of the podcast clients such as iPodder or iTunes to subscribe to your podcast, you should be prepared for those who are still using an RSS news reader. For them, let's talk about enclosure tags.

An enclosure tag is one of the optional elements that exists in RSS 2.0. Like so many elements, it provides a way to describe pieces of information beyond the basics of a story link and channel description. <enclosure> is an optional subelement of <item>. Looking back at Listing 9.1, the enclosure tag should be inserted just before the </item> tag for each episode of the podcast.

The enclosure tag has three required attributes. "url" is the location of the enclosure, "length" is the file length (in bytes), and "type" is the type of file it is, expressed as one of the standard MIME types.

```
<enclosure url="http://www.ABG2Podcasting.com/mp3s/EarlyPodcast.mp3"
length="18218340" type="audio/mpeg" />
```

Table 9.1 Mime File Types Cover Far More Than Just Audio

ai	application/postscript	**c**	text/plain
aif	audio/x-aiff	**cc**	text/plain
aifc	audio/x-aiff	**ccad**	application/clariscad
aiff	audio/x-aiff	**cdf**	application/x-netcdf
asc	text/plain	**class**	application/octet-stream
au	audio/basic	**cpio**	application/x-cpio
avi	video/x-msvideo	**cpt**	application/mac-compactpro
bcpio	application/x-bcpio	**csh**	application/x-csh
bin	application/octet-stream	**css**	text/css

Table 9.1 (continued)

dcr	application/x-director	**kar**	audio/midi
dir	application/x-director	**latex**	application/x-latex
dms	application/octet-stream	**lha**	application/octet-stream
doc	application/msword	**lsp**	application/x-lisp
drw	application/drafting	**lzh**	application/octet-stream
dvi	application/x-dvi	**m**	text/plain
dwg	application/acad	**man**	application/x-troff-man
dxf	application/dxf	**me**	application/x-troff-me
dxr	application/x-director	**mesh**	model/mesh
eps	application/postscript	**mid**	audio/midi
etx	text/x-setext	**midi**	audio/midi
exe	application/octet-stream	**mif**	application/vnd.mif
ez	application/andrew-inset	**mime**	www/mime
f	text/plain	**mov**	video/quicktime
f90	text/plain	**movie**	video/x-sgi-movie
fli	video/x-fli	**mp2**	audio/mpeg
gif	image/gif	**mp3**	audio/mpeg
gtar	application/x-gtar	**mpe**	video/mpeg
gz	application/x-gzip	**mpeg**	video/mpeg
h	text/plain	**mpg**	video/mpeg
hdf	application/x-hdf	**mpga**	audio/mpeg
hh	text/plain	**ms**	application/x-troff-ms
hqx	application/mac-binhex40	**msh**	model/mesh
htm	text/html	**nc**	application/x-netcdf
html	text/html	**oda**	application/oda
ice	x-conference/x-cooltalk	**pbm**	image/x-portable-bitmap
ief	image/ief	**pdb**	chemical/x-pdb
iges	model/iges	**pdf**	application/pdf
igs	model/iges	**pgm**	image/x-portable-graymap
ips	application/x-ipscript	**pgn**	application/x-chess-pgn
ipx	application/x-ipix	**png**	image/png
jpe	image/jpeg	**pnm**	image/x-portable-anymap
jpeg	image/jpeg	**pot**	application/mspowerpoint
jpg	image/jpeg	**ppm**	image/x-portable-pixmap
js	application/x-javascript	**pps**	application/mspowerpoint

ppt	application/mspowerpoint		**sv4crc**	application/x-sv4crc
ppz	application/mspowerpoint		**swf**	application/x-shockwave-flash
pre	application/x-freelance		**t**	application/x-troff
prt	application/pro_eng		**tar**	application/x-tar
ps	application/postscript		**tcl**	application/x-tcl
qt	video/quicktime		**tex**	application/x-tex
ra	audio/x-realaudio		**texi**	application/x-texinfo
ram	audio/x-pn-realaudio		**texinfo**	application/x-texinfo
ras	image/cmu-raster		**tif**	image/tiff
rgb	image/x-rgb		**tiff**	image/tiff
rm	audio/x-pn-realaudio		**tr**	application/x-troff
roff	application/x-troff		**tsi**	audio/TSP-audio
rpm	audio/x-pn-realaudio-plugin		**tsp**	application/dsptype
rtf	text/rtf		**tsv**	text/tab-separated-values
rtx	text/richtext		**txt**	text/plain
scm	application/x-lotusscreencam		**unv**	application/i-deas
set	application/set		**ustar**	application/x-ustar
sgm	text/sgml		**vcd**	application/x-cdlink
sgml	text/sgml		**vda**	application/vda
sh	application/x-sh		**viv**	video/vnd.vivo
shar	application/x-shar		**vivo**	video/vnd.vivo
silo	model/mesh		**vrml**	model/vrml
sit	application/x-stuffit		**wav**	audio/x-wav
skd	application/x-koan		**wrl**	model/vrml
skm	application/x-koan		**xbm**	image/x-xbitmap
skp	application/x-koan		**xlc**	application/vnd.ms-excel
skt	application/x-koan		**xll**	application/vnd.ms-excel
smi	application/smil		**xlm**	application/vnd.ms-excel
smil	application/smil		**xls**	application/vnd.ms-excel
snd	audio/basic		**xlw**	application/vnd.ms-excel
sol	application/solids		**xml**	text/xml
spl	application/x-futuresplash		**xpm**	image/x-xpixmap
src	application/x-wais-source		**xwd**	image/x-xwindowdump
step	application/STEP		**xyz**	chemical/x-pdb
stl	application/SLA		**zip**	application/zip
stp	application/STEP			
sv4cpio	application/x-sv4cpio			

The list of standard MIME types shown in Table 9.1 shows that enclosure tags can be used for more than just podcasts, but for most podcasters it will be enough to know that they can be used to allow a listener who's committed to an RSS news reader to subscribe to, and receive, the podcast. You should understand that not every RSS news reader can handle enclosures such as podcasts, but while the computer industry is still trying to figure out how to build support for RSS (and all its related media types) into operating systems and applications, a version of your RSS feed with enclosure tags may expand the potential audience for your podcast.

Thinking About Your Server

There's really good news when it comes to thinking about your server for RSS. The good news is that you don't really have to think about your server very much when it comes to an RSS feed. The XML technology that underlies RSS doesn't require anything special on the server side; from the server's point of view it's just another text file. The MP3 files that contain the podcast itself are similarly easy on the server, at least from the perspective of additional services or applications required to deliver the files to the listener. So with nothing new required, this can be a really short section, right? Well, kinda. While you don't have to run out and buy (or download, or develop) lots of new stuff for the server, there are some things that you need to keep in mind if you're going to build or populate a server for your podcasts.

The first thing to keep in mind is storage. You might have noticed that MP3 files can get rather large, especially if your podcast tends to the lengthy side. Let's say that each podcast you produce is an MP3 file that clocks in at 12 megabytes. Let's also say that you do one podcast a week. That makes 624 megabytes a year, which isn't a huge number by today's standards. If you change your assumptions to create a podcast each business day then your storage requirement for a year goes over three gigabytes. That's beginning to hit a point that becomes interesting to the people who run hosting services, especially if you're trying to run your podcast on one of the introductory or entry-level service packages.

One of the decisions you'll need to make is about the size of your archives: For how long do you want to make each podcast available? Some people decide that they want all of their podcasts available for anyone who wants to go through and "catch up," or in the case that an earlier podcast is made more relevant or interesting because of external events. Others feel that podcasts are ephemeral, "in the moment" creations that don't need to be kept for posterity. Either decision is perfectly valid, but you should understand that the decision has ramifications beyond the purely philosophical.

One of the ramifications is how you will back up your site with its podcasts. One of the earliest laws of computing is still true: Computers crash. When the server with your site and podcasts on it crashes, a current backup will allow you to be back on the Internet in the shortest time with the least disruption for your listeners. Now, it's possible to simply make copies of every page, file, and podcast before they're uploaded, and that strategy works until you have interactive features such as comments enabled for your site. If you want to have copies of all the comments on your pages, you'll need to FTP the files down to a local system before you put them onto removable media and store them somewhere your computer isn't. As your site grows, remember to figure the size of these regular backup downloads into your total bandwidth-used calculations. There's nothing like getting a nasty surprise from your safety-oriented activities to make you neglect them, and neglecting your backups is something you just shouldn't do.

Since neither the XML or MP3 files require any services or applications to be executed on your server, they don't add to the security issues that you'll need to think about. That doesn't mean that there are no security concerns at all; any time you have a computer attached to the Internet, you should be aware of the issues that exist with any operating systems or applications that you're running.

First, you should always make sure that the operating system, web server, and any other software you might be using on the server (such as a database or content management system) is up to date, patched, and properly configured. You might find it useful to subscribe to news lists, usenet groups, or RSS text feeds that concern your software. It's important to keep current with versions and patches because they are often released in response to attacks and vulnerabilities. You might think that no malicious attacker would be interested in your little podcast site, but there are those who will exploit smaller sites for the practice it gives, or to take control of a computer or file system to use as a porn or illegal download server. How could they find your system? Google is a great tool for vandals and thieves because it allows them to search for sites that contain key strings and word combinations that are common to vulnerable systems.

It's also important to make sure that you're updating *all* your software; patches and updates to one piece of software often depend on the services available in the latest version of another. If you only update part of your software, you could be missing out on critical protection from attacks.

Finally, realize that, while RSS, XML, and MP3 files don't carry any fresh vulnerability for your server, the applications that keep track of visitors, serve ads, manage your content, or automatically create an RSS feed may, in fact, increase your exposure. How? All of these services have an executable component, whether it's PERL, PHP, ASP, or another coding system. It's fine to have these; just remember that you must be extra vigilant as part of the cost of offering the added features to your visitors and listeners.

Preparing Your Podcast for Syndication

Before they get into the cockpit to take off, pilots do a pre-flight check of the airplane to make sure it's safe and ready to fly. We're ready to give your podcast to the world, but let's take just a moment to go over the details of your file and feed to make sure it's ready to go. Remember: Once you've released something on the Internet, it's impossible to completely pull it back.

Your pre-podcast checklist should include

- The MP3 File

    Take a moment to listen to the file to make sure it's the podcast you want to publish. Then take a moment to check the name of the file. Make sure there aren't any spaces in the name, and that you're very certain of the name itself.

- The ID3 Tags

    Do the tags say what you want them to say? Is the title consistent with the titles of all your podcasts? Is the copyright, author, date, and other information all correct?

- The Website

    Does the text that will accompany your podcast match the content of your recording? Is the URL that people can use to get to the podcast directly correct? Double-check the name of the MP3 file against the name you've typed into your site's HTML code. Do you want to let people make comments to your podcast? If so, are the comments turned on for your site?

- The RSS Feed

    Is the XML correct? Does the header on the RSS code correctly identify the version of RSS you're using? Are all the URLs in the RSS feed (including, most importantly, the URL for the podcast itself) correct? Finally, have you validated the RSS code using one of the available online validators? If the code isn't valid, do you know what's wrong? Can you fix it? If so, fix it and move on. If not, figure out the problem, then fix it and move on.

- Your Hosting Provider

    Are you ready for thousands of people to subscribe to your podcast? Is your hosting provider? How about your hosting company or ISP—are they ready for the onslaught? Be ready for success, and know how much bandwidth your service can provide on a monthly basis.

That's it. If all these things are in order then upload your files and get ready for your listening public. Of course, if you want lots more people to find your podcast, you'll want to list it in the big directories, but that's the next section....

Getting Listed

How do people find podcasts? There are now thousands of podcasts, with more coming into being every week, so how's the listener to know what's out there? The vast majority of podcast listeners find their podcasts through one of the major directories. Like podcasts themselves, new directories spring up, so don't be afraid to go to Google and look up podcast + directory + listing to find directories that aren't listed here in the book.

The first step toward being listed in any of the directories is to make sure that your podcast and your RSS feed are working and are correct (or validated). Most of the directories will test the information you provide; if the feed or the MP3 file don't behave as expected, they will not include your podcast in the directory, and thousands will be deprived of the opportunity to hear your great creation. Make sure that doesn't happen, and have fun getting started with the following directories:

- iTunes Music Store Podcast Directory

  https://phobos.apple.com/WebObjects/MZFinance.woa/wa/publishPodcast

  This is the new 800-pound gorilla on the block. This is the directory that links straight into iTunes; if you want your podcast seen by the masses, this is the directory to be part of.

- iPodder.org

  http://www.ipodder.org/directory/4/podcasts/contribute

  iPodder.org is one of the largest and most influential podcast sites. The directory is different than those on other sites, though, since you create your own OPML file to describe your site and link it to the other sites contained in the directory. The link given here takes you to the iPodder.org site and lets you get started on the path to learning about OPML (it's not hard) and becoming part of the iPodder.org directory.

- Podcast Alley

  http://www.podcastalley.com/add_a_podcast.php

  Asks for simple information: the name of the podcast, the URL, and a description. They confirm that the link works, and you're in. Podcast Alley is one of the older directories, and is used by many podcast listeners.

- PodcastingNews.com

  http://www.podcastingnews.com/topics/Add_Your_Podcast.html

  A site that has lots of news about podcasts as well as a directory of new podcasts. They ask for the name of your podcast, a description, and the URL of your RSS feed.

■ Podcast.net

http://www.podcast.net/addpodcast

The directory listing here has more information, so they ask for more data. Show title, host name, homepage and RSS URLs, up to three category designations, description, location, language, adult content classification, and key words (for user to search against), are all requested, and make it easier for listeners to find the podcasts that most interest them.

■ Techpodcasts.com

http://www.techpodcasts.com/addons/application/tpn-application.php

You "join" Techpodcasts.com, ascribing to their charter, and then providing basic contact info, podcast content and location information, biography, description of the show, and the schedule on which the show is released.

■ Podfeed.net

http://www.podfeed.net/add_podcast.asp

The basic information of links, description, language, and category. They validate the feed and links, then send an email to let you know you've been listed in the directory.

■ Podnova.com

http://www.podnova.com/index_for_podcasters.srf

Podnova offers a code generator to build the code behind a button you can add to your site, as well as the ability to let you add your podcast's URL to an engine that will then search and index the results.

■ GigaDial.com

http://www.gigadial.com/public/station-ae?station_name=

GigaDial allows users to see podcasts and organize them into "channels" that they can build from related podcasts into, say, a comedy channel or a technology channel. It's easy to create an entry, and interesting to use.

These directories should get you started. By the time you get through with the process of being listed in these, there will be more directories, more podcast listeners, and a larger potential audience for the podcast you've created as an Absolute Beginner.

THE ABSOLUTE MINIMUM

Public syndication is how your listeners are able to subscribe to your podcast. With a few simple lines of text, you give them the ability to let their computer keep track of when a new podcast is on your site.

An RSS (Really Simple Syndication) feed tells a piece of software (such as iPodder) where it can find your podcasts.

After you've created the RSS feed, make sure your server is safe, secure, and ready to provide your podcast to listeners. The safety and security come down to following basic common-sense rules that apply to any server that's connected to the Internet.

Have your podcast listed in the public podcasting directories. Getting your podcast listed in the directory is a simple step that can boost your traffic by leaps and bounds. Make sure your server's prepared, get your listing created, and get ready to join the podcasting community.

10

IN-HOUSE SYNDICATION

Most people who take up podcasting as a hobby care about getting their podcasts on as many MP3 players as possible. When podcasting becomes a business tool, though, suddenly the focus can turn to controlling who is able to download and listen to the podcast.

The key to controlling access is secure distribution, where you require your listeners to provide a user name and password, or you place limits on the computers that can get to the RSS feed by explicitly placing addresses or names in an access control list. While you might hear that there is no way to make an RSS feed secure, there are mechanisms to limit the distribution of a podcast to those who "need to know."

Of course, the first key to being successful with a limited-distribution podcast is understanding exactly why you want to limit those who hear, and precisely who the audience should be. Only after you figure out the answer to those questions should you go to work on your limitation strategy.

The limitation strategies can take several forms, from limiting access to a website, to requiring special login information, and even to changing the basic distribution mechanism of the podcast itself. Each strategy can serve a different business need, and a different audience.

Secure Distribution to a Targeted Audience

There are two broad paths you can take to limiting access to your podcast. The first is to place limits on the RSS feed that carries the podcast to subscribers. The second is to limit access to the website, or web page, that hosts the RSS code and the podcast file. There are advantages and disadvantages to each, so let's examine what's involved.

Controlling Access to the RSS Feed

The basic RSS feed is, of course, simply an application of XML code for allowing two computers to talk to one another. While most RSS feeds are set up to make it easy for any computer that can find the feed to get the content, RSS can also, through third-party services, be set up to require authentication, or confirmation of who the user is through a combination of user name and password.

If you're programming in RSS, you can extend your feed by adding pretty much anything you want, as long as you do it in the Namespace, one of the standard, defined XML fields that makes up an RSS feed. This assumes you're using RSS 2.0, which allows for extension through the Namespace, since using this area allows for compatibility with the earlier RSS 0.9x.

There are other options that may be available depending on the server software used by the website that hosts your RSS feed. For example, Apache allows for personalization based on a user name and password. While somewhat crude, this method can be used to authenticate a user and customize the particular podcast that they are given access to.

Your Own Private Network

A less "kludgy" method is to require users to connect to the web server through a Virtual Private Network (VPN). VPNs are almost ubiquitous in corporate computing from remote locations, since they provide both user authentication and data encryption. When you add to this the fact that VPNs are easy for a technical staff to implement because the functionality is readily available with every server operating system (and free VPN clients are available for every significant client operating system), the result is an option that may well be the most attractive for corporate and institutional podcasters who want to have control over who downloads their programs.

Of course, all the methods based on server protection assume that you have some facility with programming, and the permissions required to place applications on the server. If neither of those is true then you'll need to turn to a third-party solution for secure distribution of your podcast.

One of the best-known third-party methods of securing an RSS feed is MySmartChannels from Myst Technology. MySmartChannels is a public implementation of the Myst Web Services platform. The channels are hosted on the Myst Technology servers, and accessible only to those who have (free) accounts on MySmartChannels and meet other group criteria you can set. This public area may be all the restriction you need for your podcast, and it is a good demonstration for the commercial version of the technology, which is licensed to be used on individual servers.

When In-House Syndication Is Appropriate

Let's look at situations when an in-house syndication process is appropriate, and situations in which it's probably best to use some other form of communication.

Education

College and university professors have been some of the early adopters of podcasting for "serious" purposes. Professors or instructors can record lectures or special presentations to be downloaded by students. Distance learning and instruction in very large or over-enrolled classes can be presented to large numbers without over-burdening facilities.

Educational institutions are well positioned to limit access to class-related podcasts since so many pieces of information are already limited to students and keyed to authorization based on student ID numbers. A class website, with authentication required, can be the portal to all the online information supporting the class. The good news here is that practically no additional programming is required for the website; the simple XML code for the podcast can just be added to the page for the course, and a new educational function is in place.

Beyond colleges and universities, primary and secondary distance educational institutions as well as home-school support organizations can take advantage of podcasting to provide lectures to accompany the other materials they offer to students who can't take advantage of more conventional classrooms.

Customer Communications

Companies have long used conferences, newsletters, and websites to keep customers informed and inspire greater loyalty. Podcasting to an existing customer list, or to those customers who already have an authenticated login name on the customer support page of the corporate website, is a logical extension of these existing communications methods. With a podcast, the CEO's speech about new products or the company's new support strategies can be delivered directly to customers, rather than simply reported on in the customer-support newsletter.

FIGURE 10.1

Colleges and universities are beginning to recognize the possibilities of podcasting courses.

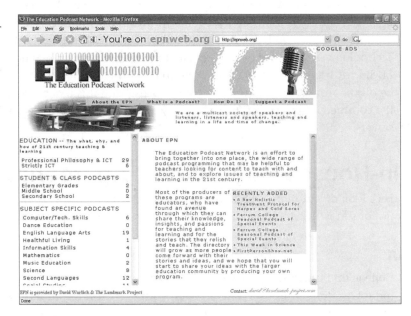

Podcasting can also increase the return on the investment a company makes in the customer meetings and conferences that take place each year. Company presentations and speeches are obvious subjects for podcasts, but customer interviews, question-and-answer sessions, and even sound-seeing tours of the exhibition hall or opening reception can add impact to podcasts on the conference.

One important factor to keep in mind (and we'll talk about this a bit more in a few pages) is that, while you can control who downloads your podcast, there's no real way to control who listens to it. Be careful about placing truly confidential information in a podcast, just as you'd be careful about putting confidential information in a newsletter.

Faith-based Organizations

Religious organizations have long embraced technology to help spread their message, and the podcast is another obvious tool for inspiring and educating people. Now, you might ask why such an organization would want to limit the listening audience for their message, but there may be many reasons for wanting listeners to register before subscribing to the podcast.

FIGURE 10.2

A secure podcast can complement other media activities for your customers.

One of the primary reasons for registering listeners of a faith-based podcast is to collect contact information for possible follow-up with additional information or support. Just as many churches and temples ask visitors for their name and address so that questions may be answered or offers of support made, the organizations may ask for registration and authentication for podcasts to enable follow-up after the content is received.

Another reason for registration and authentication might be to make content that is available only to individuals who support the organization or who have paid for a particular set of educational material. Many religious organizations have publishing arms that provide material to purchasers, and provide a podcast that must be subscribed to through financial support or other means recognized by the organization.

Political Organizations

Communicating with members and interested individuals is a constant challenge for political organizations. There are certainly plenty of opportunities for unregistered podcasts of a political nature (there are already lots of political podcasts), but an interest group or a political party may also want to communicate only with those it knows are sympathetic to its goals. A podcast can also be a way of bringing the direct words of a leader's speech to a large group of authenticated contributors or workers.

As with the podcasts from religious organizations, it may be that one of the reasons for requiring registration and authentication is to gather contact information for follow-up and future solicitation by email or paper mail. The key, as with all of the podcasts we talk about in this section, is to remember that you can control who downloads your podcast, but you can't control who listens to the podcast—be careful about precisely what information goes into the podcast you create.

FIGURE 10.3

Podcasts can be used to communicate political ideas.

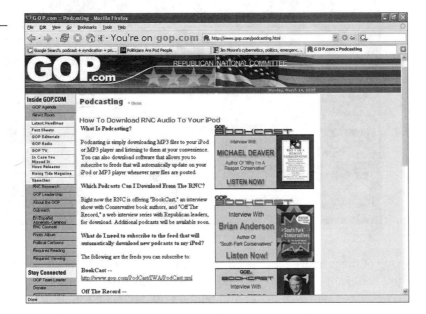

Simple In-House Syndication Strategies

The very first thing you must do when deciding to limit distribution of your podcast is to answer the question, "Why?" The answer to that question will determine not only the method you choose to protect your podcast, but the strategy you employ to promote the podcast and the materials you use to support the podcast.

The initial division in strategies comes when you decide whether your primary concern is limiting distribution to a select audience or making sure you have the information you want on the people who download your podcast. If audience restriction is of primary importance, there are steps to be taken to keep the podcast private, while a different set of steps will be of more value if gathering listener information is your main concern. Let's start with some strategies for keeping the podcast private.

Security Through Obscurity

The first step is the most elementary: It's tough for anyone to subscribe to your podcast if they don't know where it is. If you want to keep your podcast private, you start by not advertising the feed through any of the normal podcast directory sites. This will keep script-kiddies looking for a challenge away from your feed, and reduce the number of angry emails you receive from people who stumble across the podcast and are frustrated because they don't know how to subscribe.

This brings us to step number two: On the web page that hosts the podcast feed, tell people how to subscribe. If they must be employees or members of a particular organization, tell them. If they must be authorized through a user name and password that they already use for another system, tell them. Just because the podcast is private, it doesn't mean you should make it difficult for a legitimate user to listen.

When you limit access to your podcast, you should reinforce the limitations on the web page that supports the podcast feed, in all support documentation concerning the podcast, and in the ID3 tags of the MP3 file itself. Most people are honest and honorable, but they're also forgetful, so reminding them frequently of any limitations will help keep your podcast in the ears of the intended audience only.

Limits on Limitations

Finally, it bears repeating that, while you can limit access to your podcast through VPNs or third-party software such as Myst, you can't really control what happens to the MP3 file once it's been downloaded. A podcast may be many things, but it's not truly secure. Be careful about the information you include in your podcast.

If you want information on your listeners, but will allow anyone to subscribe as long as they're willing to register, then you have a different set of concerns and considerations. Many of these will be built around the fact that you're asking your listeners to give you something in exchange for the right to listen to your podcast.

Privacy Matters

One of the realities of working on the Internet today is that you must be sensitive to privacy and security concerns that your listeners will have. If you're asking for any kind of personal information as part of the registration process, you must develop a privacy policy and post it on the same page as the questionnaire that gathers registration information. It goes without saying that you must protect your listeners' private information when it's stored on your computers.

Once you've assured your listeners that their information will be safe, you must give them an incentive to part with their information—after all, there are plenty of podcasts that don't ask for anything at all in return. This is where three things come into play. First, your podcast should offer information that simply can't be had anywhere else. This could be a lecture from a well-known individual, a particular take on a religious issue, or accurate prognostications on just about anything. Whatever the content, it must be both unique and special.

Next, your podcast should be part of a system of information in which all the pieces support one another. A great podcast that's hosted on a great website that supports an interesting blog with an active community of commenters is much more likely to seem worth the risk and trouble of registration and authentication than a podcast that provides no information up front for potential listeners.

Finally, you should be very clear about requiring registration when you list your podcast on the central podcast directory sites. Unlike podcasts with a limited target audience, you'll want to list the registration-required podcasts on the directory sites in order to attract more listeners, but you want to reduce negative feelings and comments by being very clear with potential listeners that you'll be asking for more than is required by the average podcast when it's time to subscribe.

While the vast majority of podcasts are completely open, it's possible to restrict subscriptions to the RSS feed. If you understand why you're placing the restrictions and what set of actions or information you want in return, the registration and authentication process can become part of a positive interaction between listener and podcast, rather than a pain in the posterior for the people you want to fill out your audience.

> **tip**
>
> One of the important rules for protecting customer information is to never collect data you don't need. Don't ask a listener for information unless you have a very good idea of how you're going to use that information. Respect the privacy and security of your listeners.

THE ABSOLUTE MINIMUM

It's not common to restrict distribution of your podcast, but it is possible. You may be able to use customization functions within your web server software, virtual private networks (VPNs), or commercial software such as MySmartChannels from Myst Technology to require registration and authentication of your listeners.

There are a variety of topic areas and podcasts for which authentication may be the right answer. Educational institutions, religious organizations, and the customer-service team within sales organizations may also find that a podcast limited to members or customers is valuable.

It's critical that you know why you're collecting registration information and what you plan to do with it. Customer information is too valuable to just keep "lying around" without a clear agenda for using the data for "legitimate purposes."

PART IV

Day-to-Day Issues You'll Face As a Podcaster

11

PROMOTING YOUR PODCAST

Whether you're in podcasting as a business undertaking or as a labor of love, it's still important to reach as many of your target listeners as possible. Podcasting provides the technological vehicle to potentially reach listeners all over the world. To turn the potential into a reality, you've got to let the world know that your podcast exists.

In this chapter, you'll learn the easiest, most effective strategies and tactics for promoting your podcast—regardless of the size of your promotional budget. After all, podcasting is considerably more fun when you know there are lots of people listening!

Get Your Podcast Listed

Remember back in Chapter 1: We were talking about finding interesting podcasts to subscribe to and we mentioned that the place to start was with the directory maintained by iPodder.org. Just as you began your quest for interesting podcasts with the iPodder directory, so will many of your potential listeners start there, also. As a result, the first and most basic step to promote your podcast is to make sure it's there when potential listeners are browsing through iPodder. Keep in mind, though, that while iPodder may be the most authoritative podcast directory out there, it's certainly not the only one. You'll want to be listed in as many as possible.

Podcast directories differ considerably when it comes to how listings are accepted. For some directories, once you've filled out their online form, you're in. For others, there is some degree of human interaction. iPodder, for example, has volunteer editors who are responsible for the listings in each category.

Getting Listed in iPodder

Let's begin your promotional efforts right now by getting your podcast listed in the iPodder directory. Begin by going to the home page at ipodder.org. As you scroll down, on the right side of the page you'll notice a column that contains the various major categories into which podcasts are assigned, as illustrated in Figure 11.1.

FIGURE 11.1
iPodder categories are listed in a column on the home page alongside corresponding file folder icons.

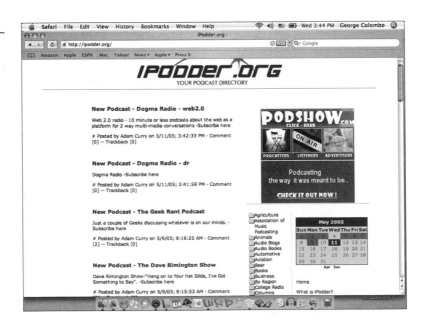

Look through the column and find the category into which your podcast will most closely fit. You shouldn't have too much trouble finding an appropriate category. As of this writing, there are 69 major podcast categories and more are being added all the time. When you find the right category, click on the file folder icon next to it.

At this point, you might possibly see another column of category names and file folder icons. That means that the category you selected is further divided into sub-categories. If that's the case, once again select the one that fits best and click on the file folder next to it.

You will arrive, finally, at a current list of podcasts in the category (or subcategory) in which you want to be listed. Each podcast will have a small icon of a globe accompanying it. At the bottom of the list, you'll find the name of the category editor, some statistical information about the category, and a link that says, "Suggest a link." Click on this link and you'll come to a form like the one in Figure 11.2. Filling out this form is all you have to do to get your podcast listed.

FIGURE 11.2

This short form is your ticket to a listing on iPodder, the most used directory of podcasts on the Internet.

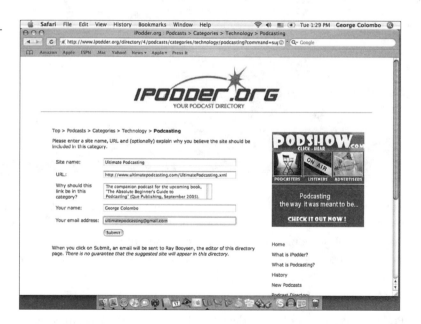

The folks at iPodder point out that there's no guarantee your listing in the directory will be accepted, but they have no interest in arbitrarily curtailing listings. They're primarily interested in making sure that the information in the directory is credible and useful for users.

Once you've filled out the form, click the Submit button. That's it; you're done! Your listing in the iPodder directory will be posted as soon as it's cleared by the category editor.

Podcast Alley

The next significant directory listing you'll want is in Podcast Alley. Let's get started with your listing there by pointing your browser to podcastalley.com.

At the top of the home page, you'll notice a link that says "Add a Podcast." Click on that link and, once again, you'll be taken to a form. This time, it will look like the one in Figure 11.3.

FIGURE 11.3

Podcast Alley will add your podcast to its directory when you provide the basic information for your listing.

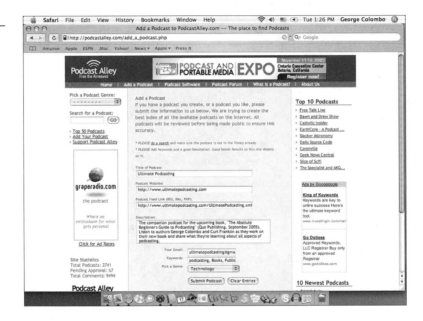

More than any other podcasting site on the Internet, Podcast Alley has evolved into the meeting and greeting place for the podcast community. Your inclusion in this directory will get your podcast exposure among the podcast community's movers and shakers (not to mention many media outlets doing research on podcasting).

iPodderX.org

iPodder X is the last of the independent first-tier directories in which you'll want to be included. Currently, iPodder X is targeted primarily at the Macintosh community, although it has announced plans to broaden its reach into the world of Windows users. Even so, Macintosh users are a disproportionately large segment of the podcast-listening population, so taking the time to make sure you're listed in this directory is well worth your time.

Beyond the First-tier Directories

The iPodder and Podcast Alley directories are two of the most visible listings you can secure for your podcast but there are several others, as well. Since registering your podcast is free, there's no reason not to register in as many directories as you can find. Beyond the two top-tier directories, here are several others you should visit:

- http://www.podcastdirectory.com
- http://www.penguinradio.com/podcasting/
- http://www.podcast.net
- http://www.podcastingnews.com
- http://www.castregister.com
- http://www.digitalpodcast.com
- http://www.podcastpickle.com

One final directory-type site that deserves your attention is Podshow.com. Although the details of this offering from Adam Curry are not public at the time of this writing, the general direction of Podshow has been discussed by Adam and his partner, Ron Bloom (most notably in a legendary two-hour podcast that roiled the podcasting community in May of 2005).

The general design of Podshow includes an entry-level tier with a bundled set of free services for neophyte podcasters. Podshow will integrate with CastBlaster to make the podcast creation process as seamless as possible. (CastBlaster is a software package for creating podcasts, published by the same people who run PodShow.) PodShow also promises to open up its design to other applications, allowing for similar integration. The overall concept is end-to-end integration for the beginning podcaster.

For the more serious podcaster, Podshow has promised a more robust set of offerings designed to support podcasts that have progressed past the point of "casual" podcasting. For many brand-new podcasters, Podshow.com (shown in Figure 11.4) will likely be an appealing, "one-stop-shopping environment" solution that facilitates the entire podcasting process end-to-end.

FIGURE 11.4

PodShow.com is positioned as a nexus for podcasters, listeners, and advertisers.

Tap into the Podcasting Community

Let's review where we are in the process right now: You've tested and then launched a podcast. Your show is available on the Web with a working RSS feed. You're updating your show regularly.

Congratulations! You are now officially a podcaster. You're a member of the club. While there's still lots to learn, you've progressed beyond basic training and—at the risk of mixing a metaphor—you're playing in the big leagues.

Now that you're officially part of the community, there are plenty of good reasons to get involved with your fellow podcasters. And, while the promotional value of getting involved in the community is obvious, it's equally obvious that the benefits of getting involved will extend far beyond the purely promotional.

Hang Out Around Podcasting's Virtual Water Cooler

The unofficial "water cooler" for much of the podcasting community is the forum section on Podcast Alley. Just go to PodcastAlley.com and select Podcast Forum from the menu bar. From there, you'll arrive at a page like the one in Figure 11.5. You'll find forums for both listeners and podcasters.

Participating in both types of forums can be helpful. The podcaster forums include a wealth of information and experience about podcasting issues out in "the real world." The listener forums are an important gauge of listener tastes and preferences.

FIGURE 11.5

There are Podcast Alley forums for both podcasters and listeners.

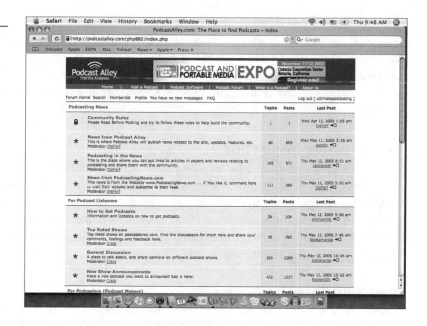

AN IMPORTANT CAVEAT ABOUT FORUMS

The forums you find on Podcast Alley and other similar sites can be an important tool for getting connected to the podcasting community. It's important to keep in mind, though, that forum participants are not a truly representative sampling of the podcasting community. For example, "early adopters" are sometimes represented disproportionately. By all means, listen to what's going on but don't forget that you're tapping in to a self-selected subset of the podcasting community.

Of course, Podcast Alley isn't the only forum for podcasters. A couple of other notable forums can be found at these web addresses:

- http://groups.yahoo.com/group/podcasters/
- http://podcastrigs.net/forum/

Participating in forums is a great idea for a number of reasons. The following sections discuss several things the forums can help you with.

Reduce Your Learning Curve

Whatever you want to do with your podcast—and the list of options seems endless—someone else has probably been there and done that (or, at least, something similar). One of the most striking things about the podcasting community is its willingness to embrace newcomers and share information. As a fledgling podcaster, this is a tremendous advantage for you. You'll be able to benefit from the collective knowledge of a smart and talented community.

Learn Best Practices

Typically, technology offers new podcasters numerous options for accomplishing each step of the podcasting process but not all of these options are equally effective. As practices, procedures, and equipment for podcasting improve, your participation in podcasting's online communities will keep you up to speed on the best options out there.

Get Creative Inspiration

The podcasting community is incredibly diverse and creative. If you don't have a large staff to help create your podcasts every week, having access to ideas and feedback from a community like this may be the next best thing. Participate in online podcasting communities so you can find out what's going on out there. Get involved and allow yourself to be challenged. And, finally, become part of the community as a vehicle to get your creative juices going.

Pay Your Dues by Giving Back

There's an old joke in the world of technology that the definition of "expert" is a guy who's a chapter ahead of you in the manual. That's certainly true in the world of podcasting. You might still be picking the brains of other podcasters but if you've reached this point in this book and understand most of the things we've covered, then—believe it or not—you're not that far from being an expert yourself.

Be as generous as you can with your time when you encounter aspiring podcasters who don't yet know as much about podcasting as you do. Show them some of the tips and techniques that you've picked up already. You'll enjoy the benefit of goodwill along with a growing reputation of expertise. (And, of course, tell everyone to pick up a copy of *The Absolute Beginner's Guide to Podcasting*. They'll thank you for it.)

Gain Exposure to Centers of Influence

Okay, after all of that, we've *finally* come to the purely promotional aspect of getting involved in the podcasting community. One great way to get your podcast exposed to potential listeners is to piggyback on someone else's audience. There's an effective way to do this and there's an ineffective way. We highly recommend the former.

Over time, as you participate in the podcasting community, your colleagues in the various forums will begin to know who you are and what you do. They'll learn about the focus and quality of your shows. And, when it's appropriate, they will tell their listeners about you. Your penetration will grow as a result of your exposure to established podcasters who act as centers of influence in the community.

In addition to your exposure to centers of influence in podcasting forums, there are two other specific tactics you can employ.

Create and Distribute Promos For Your Show

Show promos are brief (around 30 seconds, usually) commercials for your podcast that are played on other people's podcasts. Adam Curry has turned promos into an art form and has regularly featured them on his *Daily Source Code* show.

Because of its popularity, *Daily Source Code* receives a tremendous number of promos and plays as many as possible in every show. There are also many other popular podcasts that play promos, too, and some may match your target audience even more closely than *DSC*.

A QUICK TUTORIAL ON CREATING GREAT PROMOS

In many ways, your single greatest promotional vehicle for your show are the promos you create. There are numerous creative approaches to creating a promo but if you want it to be effective—that is, drive listeners to your podcast—then your promo must be engaging, memorable, and personal.

Engaging means that you find something that can grab your listener's attention quickly and "hook" him or her for the duration of the promo. Music, humor, intrigue...something that grabs the listener by the collar and doesn't let go for 30 seconds or so. (Hint: If you do nuance, your promo is not the best place to showcase that particular talent.)

Memorable means that you find something that sticks in your listener's mind or is triggered there later on. Certainly, you'll want to give your podcast as memorable name as possible. If your podcast is commercial and you have a website, it should be the same name as your podcast and should be repeated in your promo multiple times.

Your promos will be much more effective if you personalize them for the podcaster who will be playing them. Don't forget, your promo is being played for that podcaster's audience—a group that, by definition, likes and/or respects the show host. When you personalize a promo, it grabs your listener's attention and piggybacks a bit on that host's goodwill with his or her audience.

Record Show Intros for Your Favorite Podcast

Another popular promotional vehicle is the creation of intros for other podcasters. These are the brief clips that are sometimes played at the beginning of a podcast that usually go something like this: "I'm Curt Franklin from *Ultimate Podcasting*. I listen to The Point podcast by Paul Figgiani and you should, too. And now, here's Paul Figgiani..."

If you create something that's funny, outrageous, or otherwise striking, then there's a chance that your favorite podcast might use it.

Promote Podcasting

As you read this, podcasting is still at the very beginning of a long and strong growth curve. Helping to support that growth curve is a powerful strategy for all podcasters to employ.

Unlike radio, podcasters are not competitively positioned against each other for the same audience. If you're on the radio during morning drive time and I'm on the radio in the same market and at the same time, then you and I have to fight for every last percentage of a ratings point. Radio is what economists refer to as a zero-sum game. If you and I are both podcasters, however, my success doesn't depend on your failure. Quite the opposite, in fact. If you're doing something interesting and I acknowledge and recommend it, the overall market for podcasting expands as the number of regular listeners grows.

So, in addition to promoting your own show, be an ambassador for podcasting. Some of the most visible podcasters in the business make this a key part of their promotional program. They do it because it works for them. And it will work for you, too.

Nail Down Your Niche

We've discussed this before but it's a point that's so important it's worth mentioning again: Where broadcasting is broad and unfocused, podcasting at its most effective is very focused and very specific. From a promotional point of view, appealing to a specific audience is a very good thing indeed. When your audience is specific, it's usually easier to find and it's almost always easier to craft an effective message.

Think back for a moment on the work you did back in Chapter 2, "Guidelines for Designing a Killer Podcast," on defining your listeners. Not only was that work valuable when it came to designing your show, it's also extremely valuable now that it's time to promote your show.

Based on what you know about your listeners, can you make some educated guesses about

- What they read
- What other podcasts they might listen to
- What conferences or conventions they attend

Since you've already done a great deal of work defining your audience, the answers to these questions ought to be relatively easy. Those answers, now, will allow you to develop some specific low-cost/high-impact promotional efforts for your podcast. (For the purposes of this discussion, we're going to assume that your promotional budget is somewhere between small and nonexistent.)

Let's take a look at how what you know about your listeners can translate into promotional strategies:

- If you know which publications your listeners read—both online and offline—then you can contact the editors at those publications. For example, if your podcast is aimed at owners of older homes who are renovating, then you might contact *Homebuilding & Renovating Magazine* (which also has a website). You might be able to write an article for them in exchange for a byline that includes a link to your podcast.

■ If your listeners are likely to be listening to a particular podcast, you might approach the producer of that podcast to explore the possibility of exchanging promos for each other's shows.

■ If there is a particular show or conference your listeners attend, you could approach the conference promoters with an arrangement to become the "official" podcast for the conference. You might provide podcasted content to show attendees in exchange for visibility among a group that closely matches your listener profile.

■ If there are organizations that your listeners belong to—either personally or professionally—then you should be active in those organizations.

These are just some examples of ideas of using your listener profile as the basis for low-cost promotional efforts for your podcast. But the number and variety of opportunities are only limited by your imagination. The guiding principle for all of your promotional efforts is to earn prominence and visibility in the niche your podcast is aimed at.

The Power of Public Relations

There is nothing that confers interest and credibility in your podcast quite as effectively as being featured in the media. For the same reasons that promoting yourself to a niche is easier than unfocused promotions (as we just saw), your focused public relations efforts will also be easier.

There are existing publications that target the same audience you're targeting with your podcast. You should be in the habit of regularly letting these publications know what you're doing.

Make contact with these publications and study their websites. Find out for each publication the best way to submit press releases, including the best timing for deadlines, the best format, and the type of content they're most often looking for. Learn enough about each publication—and chances are that there aren't too many in your niche—and get in the habit of thinking about the specific type of content that will appeal to each one.

Some publications and many websites will want press releases. Whenever you're doing something interesting or noteworthy with your podcast, it's worthwhile to send out a press release. If you're not sure how to format the release, someone at the publication can tell you what they're looking for.

Sometimes, trade publications will be looking for short articles to publish over your byline and bio (see promotional strategies discussed previously). If you do audio essays on your podcast, the content can easily be re-purposed into an essay for publication.

Still others will be looking for a ready, ongoing source for quotes and comments. In these cases, make sure you're identified as a podcast producer and that the name of your podcast is used.

THE ABSOLUTE MINIMUM

You'll enjoy podcasting a great deal more when you know that lots of people are listening. Targeted promotional efforts can provide a great return on your effort.

- Promoting your podcast begins with getting it listed in the various podcast directories, including iPodder.org and PodcastAlley.com.

- The online podcasting community can provide you with a wealth of resources—including visibility.

- Your podcast targets a specific, identifiable group of people. Your promotional efforts should be focused on that community.

- Public relations can be used effectively within your niche. The key is to provide each publication with the type of content it wants.

12

DOUBLE-ENDERS: THE SECRET TECHNIQUE FOR REMOTE INTERVIEWS

Podcasts are about conversation. However, some conversations are more difficult to record than others. In this chapter, you'll learn an insider's secret for getting pristine sound quality when you record a conversation that takes place over the phone.

The Insiders' Secret Technique for Remote Interviews

If you're like most podcasters, your podcast probably involves you talking to other people from time to time. Perhaps you want to record an interview with an author or some other type of expert or celebrity. Or maybe there's someone who co-hosts your podcast or, at least, appears on it regularly. Maybe all of these situations apply to you at different times. In any event, chances are that you're regularly going to encounter situations where you'll want to record your conversation with someone else.

Ideally, the person you want to chat with will be able to join you in your studio and you'll both sit down in front of a microphone to record the conversation. If that's not possible, your fallback position might possibly be to record the conversation on location with portable recording equipment. That's not necessarily ideal but the results can be perfectly acceptable.

Sometimes, though, you're going to want to record a conversation with someone when it's simply not possible for the two of you to be in the same room at the same time. This is when things can get a little dicey.

STRAIGHTFORWARD RECORDING TECHNIQUES (THAT DON'T REALLY WORK VERY WELL)

Most podcasters' first inclination for addressing this problem was to conduct their conversation over the Internet using a technology known as VoIP, or Voice Over Internet Protocol. The solution of choice was a free Internet telephony service called Skype (skype.com). In theory, this ought to be a great solution since VoIP dictates that a Skype conversation takes place in a digital format. That means it ought to be a relatively simple matter to capture the digital stream with recording software.

In practice, though, the quality of the connection can often be inconsistent and sometimes it's downright poor. Moreover, holding a VoIP conversation while recording it simultaneously can overtax the processing power of your computer. In fact, we've experimented extensively with this approach and often wound up with results that were reminiscent of the old *Max Headroom* television show.

Another option is to record a conversation from a standard telephone connection. There are a number of ways to accomplish this. A company called JK Audio (www.jkaudio.com) offers several interface devices—some of which are relatively inexpensive—that will facilitate the recording of phone conversations.

Depending on how you choose to record the conversation, one or both of the parties will produce a relatively low-quality recording. (Think about the sound quality of the callers on your favorite talk radio show and you'll have an idea of the level of quality we're talking about.) This is certainly a more reliable approach than recording from Skype and the sound quality will do in a pinch. Ultimately, though, quality-conscious podcasters find the sound quality to be generally unsatisfactory if not necessarily unacceptable.

There is technique, however, that is surprisingly simple to do and reliably produces outstanding results. If both you and the person you're talking to have computers that can record sound, then you're in business! This technique—long an insider's secret in the broadcast industry—is known as a double-ender. It's so simple that you can use it for a short interview with a relatively un-technical interview subject but it's robust enough that you and a remote co-host can record entire shows with it. We guarantee that the first time you use this technique, you'll be astonished at the results.

In a nutshell, a *double-ender* means that each end of a conversation is recorded separately. Then, when the conversation is over, the two recordings are stitched together in a way that's completely transparent to the listener. Of course, that simple description doesn't quite give you all the information you need, so let's take a look at a step-by-step explanation of how to produce a double-ender.

Recording Your Double-Ender

For the purposes of our explanation, we'll say that you are producing the podcast that's going to include the double-ender. Both you and the person you'll be interviewing need to get ready to record individually. That means that each of you must have the following items available and ready to use:

- A computer
- Recording software
- A microphone

In addition, you'll both need to have a telephone available.

As the podcast producer, you should be using recording software that can accommodate multiple track recording. That's not necessary for the person you're interviewing, though.

In fact, if the person you're interviewing doesn't use audio recording regularly then he or she can probably get away with using the microphone that's built into the computer. Of course, a separate mic—or at least a headset with a built-in microphone—will always produce a better-quality recording.

With those basic items under control, you and your recording partner can follow these steps to complete this part of the process.

Eliminate As Much Ambient Noise As Possible

Try to make sure the rooms in which you're both recording are as quiet as possible. Not only will this yield raw recordings with better quality, but it will also give you much more flexibility later on when it's time to mix and edit.

Pay particular attention to ambient noise, the "white noise" that's part of every environment. Fans or air conditioners are common culprits when it comes to generating this sort of noise.

Check Your Recording Levels

By now, you're familiar with the whole process of making sure you're recording at appropriate levels. It's possible, however, that the person you'll be talking to doesn't share your expertise. If that's the case then take a few moments to step them through the process. (It will be helpful if you're familiar with the recording software they're using.)

Your recording partner's level needs to be adequate but not to the point of over modulating. (It's easier to increase their volume level later on, if necessary, but you can't remove the distortion that over modulating will cause.) If possible, have the other person do a short test recording to make sure that everything's working properly and levels are set appropriately.

Get Connected on the Phone

This is just as straightforward as it sounds. One of you will call the other one up and you'll get ready to conduct a simple conversation over the phone.

Make sure that you can hear each other clearly. Also, make certain that you can both talk on the phone comfortably without anyone bumping his or her phone into the microphone!

Hit the Record Button and Start Talking

At this point, when you and your recording partner are ready to begin your conversation, each of you can hit the Record button and you can get started. It's not even necessary to count down in order to synchronize your recordings. (As the podcast's producer, you'll take care of synchronizing the recordings shortly.)

Now, all you have to do is finish your conversation and stop recording when you're done. You'll wind up with a recording of just your end of the conversation, as shown in Figure 12.1.

Save Your Partner's Recording in an Appropriate Format

The specific steps for this part of the process will vary, depending on the recording software your partner is using. If he or she can export audio to an MP3 file, that would be ideal. If that's not possible then any standard file format (.wav, aiff, and so on) will generally do. MP3 is preferable only because it produces smaller files.

FIGURE 12.1

You now have a recording of your half of the conversation. Notice the gaps where your partner was doing the talking.

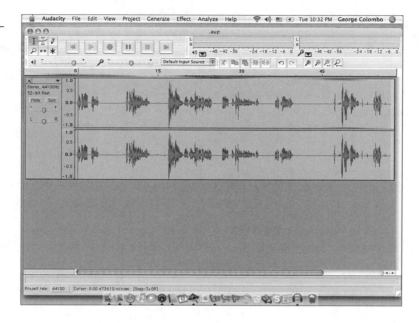

Don't sacrifice audio quality by trying to reduce the size of your MP3 file with a lower sample rate. An MP3 file with a high sample rate will still produce a file that's considerably smaller than any of the uncompressed formats, but it will yield much better results in the final mix.

Transferring Files That Are Too Large for Email

The next step is to get your partner's exported audio file onto your computer. If your recording consists of a short interview then this step is as simple as sending the file as an email attachment.

If the conversation was a bit longer, however, you're going to run into an apparent roadblock. Most email systems have built in constraints on the size of the files they'll accept. Even Google's Gmail—renowned for its generous capacity—will only allow email messages of 10 Megabytes or smaller. Even a moderately long audio recording will easily exceed that limit.

While you can certainly use FTP software if you have access to FTP space on the Web, there is a simpler way around this constraint. A website called YouSendIt (www.yousendit.com) offers a free service that will allow you to send and receive files of up to one gigabyte. From the YouSendIt home page, your recording partner can follow the onscreen instructions for sending the file to you, as shown in Figure 12.2.

Shortly after the file is sent, you'll receive an email with a link that will allow you to download it, bypassing both your partner's email system and yours. Click on the link and you'll have your partner's audio file on your hard drive in a few moments, ready to be imported into your audio software.

FIGURE 12.2

Sending large
files with
YouSendIt is
simple and
straightforward.

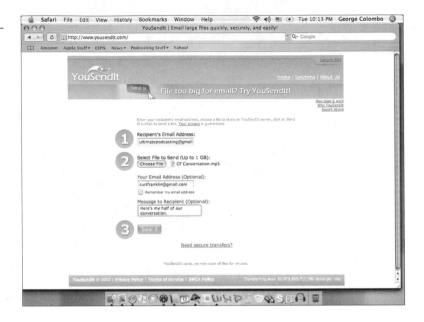

FIGURE 12.2

Sending large files with YouSendIt is simple and straightforward.

SENDING LARGE FILES IN REAL TIME

When you're transferring a large file from one person to another and both people are online simultaneously, an easy and straightforward technique is to use instant messaging software. All of the standard instant messaging clients (such as AOL Instant Messenger, Yahoo Messenger, Skype, and so on) allow you to send very large files between users as long as they're both online at the same time.

Mixing Your Double-Ender

Now, import the audio you just received from your partner into your audio software. You'll wind up with two tracks of audio, as shown in Figure 12.3.

Chances are, you'll wind up with a result like this. Without even hitting the Play button on your software, you can see that the two tracks are not aligned properly. If you listen right now, you'll hear the voices of you and your recording partner talking over each other.

Not to worry, though. Your recording software has a tool that will allow you to shift each track separately. Fixing the problem is as simple as shifting one of the tracks over until the audio in one track is aligned with the gaps in the other track, meshing with each other just like two adjoining gears. You can make the rough adjustment visually, then fine tune the alignment by ear.

When you're done, you'll wind up with two perfectly aligned tracks like the ones you see in Figure 12.4.

FIGURE 12.3

Both halves of the conversation have been imported into your program, but something's not quite right yet.

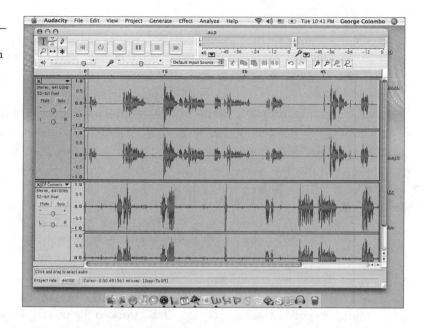

FIGURE 12.4

No one will be able to tell that you and your partner were not together when this was recorded.

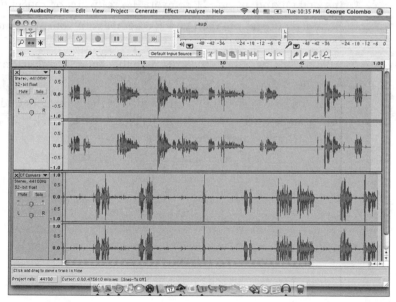

Other than possibly adjusting the relative volume levels of the two tracks, you're done! The beauty of recording a double-ender is that you're able to align the two tracks in their entirety simply by sampling and working with a small section. Once you've properly aligned a small section of the two tracks, the rest of the tracks will be perfectly aligned no matter how long they are. You can align a 45-minute conversation merely by sampling and aligning a 10-second segment!

When you're done, no one will be able to tell that you and your recording partner weren't in the same room. (And believe us: If you're podcasting long enough, someday you'll wind up interviewing someone you'll be glad to not be in the same room with!) You can even co-host a podcast with someone in a different city and no one need ever know.

Double-enders are incredibly simple but the result they produce is nothing short of remarkable. This is a genuine insider's secret, so don't tell anyone...but feel free to suggest that they buy a copy of this book!

THE ABSOLUTE MINIMUM

- The double-ender technique will allow you to record high quality conversations even when the person you're talking to is somewhere else.

- Recording a double-ender starts with each person recording his or her part of a conversation separately.

- When both audio tracks have been recorded, the person who is not producing the podcast sends his or her audio track to the person doing the producing and mixing, using FTP software, IM software, or YouSendIt.com.

- Both audio tracks are then joined together with your standard mixing software.

- Aligning the two audio tracks of a double-ender is simple and straightforward.

- After you've adjusted the relative levels of the two tracks and mixed them into a single track, your listeners will not be able to tell that the two parties were not in the same room.

13

GENERATING INCOME WITH YOUR PODCAST

Maybe you're only looking to generate enough revenue with your podcast to offset some of your hosting and bandwidth expenses. Or, perhaps, you want to turn your podcast into a full-time undertaking that generates enough income to pay the bills. In either case—or if your objectives lie somewhere in between—this chapter will show you how to start generating income with your podcast.

Get Ready to Generate Revenue

Even if you're not looking to get rich from your podcast, we're confident you wouldn't mind generating some income from the hours you'll be putting into show prep, recording, and post-production. There are several business models for generating revenue that are available to you. They are

- The Associate/Affiliate Model
- Donations
- The Sponsorship Model
- Distribution to Paid Subscriber

In this chapter, we're going to explore all of these models and help you decide which one is best for you. Before we do, however, there are a few points you'll want to consider.

Podcasting is an emerging technology. It's still developing and jockeying for its place in the wider panoply of communications media. Even so, as a communications and entertainment medium, it shares some fundamental characteristics with radio, television, magazines, and even newspapers. While we don't yet know all of the specifics of how podcasting's economics will evolve over time, we do know enough to share with you some principles about how to generate revenue with your podcasts.

It would be wonderful if we could tell you that it's possible to generate income based primarily on the value of the content you create. Unfortunately, that simply isn't realistic (with one exception we'll discuss shortly). In this way, podcasting is just like every other communications medium. No matter how terrific your content is, it will take some additional effort to turn it into revenue.

In fact, regardless of the business model you eventually adopt, there are two essential steps you'll need to take first:

Build Up Your Audience

For those of you who podcast in Latin, we'll begin by saying that building as large an audience as possible is the *sine qua non* of generating revenue. If you don't podcast in Latin, we'll simply note that the more successful you are at attracting and retaining listeners, the better positioned you'll be to generate revenue. With lots of listeners, you'll have multiple means of generating revenue at your disposal...and, with enough listeners, it will be almost impossible to avoid making money. With few listeners, your income options will be severely constrained regardless of the quality of your content or the creativity you bring to the business side of your podcasting endeavors.

When you're ready to begin making money as a podcaster, then, the first thing you'll want to do is go back and re-read the chapter on promoting your podcast.

Pay particular attention to the strategies for promoting your podcast to the niche at which it's aimed. You'll want to understand these strategies intimately. Beyond understanding them, you'll need to implement them.

Promoting your podcast needs to be on your agenda every single day. Unfortunately, there is no magic technique to gain a hundred new listeners to your podcast. However, there are probably 50 techniques for gaining a couple of new listeners—and you'll want to use every one of them.

In addition to growing your audience, some of the business models you might want to pursue will require you to document your audience. If you decide that one of these business models is right for you, then you'll want to structure the distribution of your podcast in a way that provides as much documentation of your audience as possible. For example, syndication services such as Feed Burner provide you with usage statistics that are more credible than the statistics you'd be able to generate by hosting your RSS feed yourself.

Never be satisfied with the number of listeners your podcast attracts and never stop your efforts to find new listeners. Your revenue opportunities will increase exponentially as the size of your audience increases.

Understand Precisely Who's Listening

The second preliminary step you'll need to take before you start generating revenue is to learn as much as you can about exactly who is listening to your podcast. Knowing who your audience is will allow you to make better decisions about revenue opportunities you might choose to pursue. In addition, if you decide you're going to pursue sponsorship arrangements (which we'll discuss shortly), you'll be able to use this information to convince potential sponsors of the value of sponsoring your podcast.

Some podcasts are inherently well positioned to do this, at least to a certain extent. For example, the popular podcast *MacCast* has an audience that is composed primarily of owners of Apple Macintosh computers. The very nature of the podcast contributes to an understanding of its audience. Other podcasts are not as well positioned and will, as a result, have to work a bit harder to unearth listener information.

If your podcast doesn't inherently define its audience as *MacCast* does, you'll have to be proactive in getting the information you want. A great tool for doing this is an online survey.

Online surveys can be administered on your website or you can solicit participants through email. If you don't have email addresses for your listeners—and most podcasters don't—then you can simply ask for volunteers in your podcast. You might tell your listeners, "We're trying to learn a little bit about our audience so that we can improve our podcast and meet the needs of our listeners more closely. If you'd like to participate in a brief online survey, drop me an email and I'll send you an initiation."

The responses you'll get will be self-selected, with means that the listeners who respond are not necessarily exactly representative of your entire audience. While that's not an ideal situation, it's also true that having some information from a self-selected sample is still better than having no information at all.

The type of information you'll want to obtain will depend on the type of podcast you produce. For example, if your podcast is about cooking then information about your listeners' computer configurations will be of limited value. On the other hand, if your podcast is technical in nature, then information about your listeners' computer habits can be valuable indeed.

Here are some things you might want to ask your listeners about:

- Age
- Listening habits (How often they listen, where they listen, and so on)
- Computer platform
- Use of portable music player
- Other information that's specific to the subject matter of your podcast

When you're ready to send out a survey, you can use email and tabulate the results yourself, but that can be tedious, time consuming, and prone to error. Another option is to use an online survey service like Zoomerang, shown in Figure 13.1.

FIGURE 13.1

At Zoomerang. com, you'll find tools that will allow you to create online surveys to learn about your listeners.

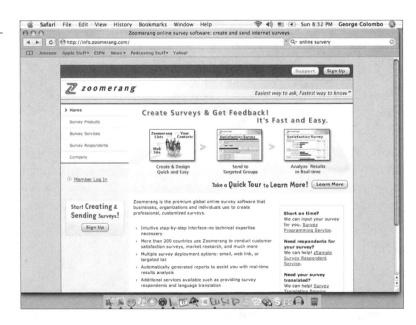

Zoomerang allows you to survey up to 100 listeners for free. You can design your survey questions and send them out to a list of respondents you select. When the surveys have been completed, Zoomerang will accumulate and analyze the results.

Okay, you're promoting your podcast as vigorously as possible and have accumulated as much data as you can about who is listening. Now, it's time to take a look at the specific ways you can start generating revenue.

Four Basic Revenue Models

There are four basic revenue models you can pursue. The first two models can be used separately or together. The third model is somewhat—but not entirely—compatible with the other two. Using the fourth model will generally preclude the use of the other three.

The Associate/Affiliate Model

Affiliate programs allow you to sell products to your listeners from your website and receive a commission. For most podcasters, this will be the revenue model of choice. It has a number of inherent advantages over the other approaches you might use:

- It doesn't require you to sell anything.
- You can begin generating revenue immediately.
- It doesn't have the negative connotations that some people attach to other methods.
- It allows you to deliver added value to your listeners.

The most popular affiliate program—by far—is the one offered by Amazon.com. An association with the largest bookseller on the Internet is a natural one for podcasters. After all, regardless of which topics you cover in your podcast, there are certainly books that are directly relevant. Beyond books, Amazon offers a range of products that is so large and diverse, it's virtually certain that you can find products to offer for sale that specifically relate to your audience's interests and needs.

When you become an Amazon Associate, you're supplied with an identifier that you can add to links to Amazon products that you feature on your website. When one of your listeners buys one of those products, you get a commission of up to 10 percent of the price of that product. In addition, you will receive a commission on anything else your listener buys from Amazon if they visit the site through one of your links.

To join the Amazon program, go to the home page at Amazon.com. Scroll to the very bottom of the page and you'll find a link that says "Join Associates." Click that link and follow the instructions you'll find onscreen. You'll be asked to create an Amazon account if you don't already have one. (If you do, your Amazon Associate account can be linked with your existing account.) You'll then be asked for information that will facilitate payments to you (such as your address and your tax I.D. or Social Security information) as well as information about your website.

Once your account has been set up, you're ready to start offering products on your website. The Amazon Associates website steps you through the process of building links and automatically generates HTML code that can be copied and pasted on to your website. As you can see in Figure 13.2, you're able to build links to specific products or you can create links based on product categories or keywords.

FIGURE 13.2

The Amazon Associates website allows you to build links to any product that Amazon offers.

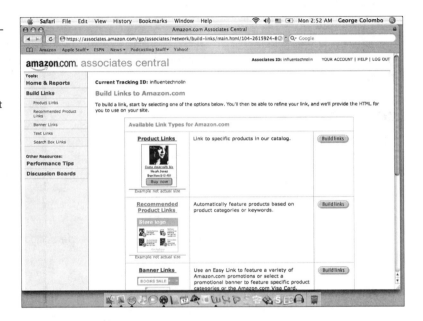

Once you're enrolled in the program, the revenue generation opportunities are virtually endless. If your podcast is focused on a specific topic, you can offer your listeners books and other products that relate to that topic. In addition, whenever you mention a specific book or product on your podcast, you can offer it for sale, too. (Links to specific books are usually created by referencing the book's ISBN number. That's a unique identifier that every book has. A great way to get started is by creating a link to ISBN number 0789734559. Try it and see how it works!)

Amazon's product catalog is so large that finding suitable products to sell will always be easy. You won't ever have to offer anything that's inappropriate merely for the sake of making money.

Moreover, this approach to generating revenue represents a real value to your listeners. Chances are, if you're talking about a book or other product, it's something that your listeners will at least be interested in learning more about. Rather than having to remember the name of a product and then having to search for information about it, they'll simply be able to go to your website and find what they're looking for. You'll have created an opportunity to generate revenue while serving your listeners' best interests at the same time.

Donations

The most widely implemented strategy for generating revenue is also the simplest: Ask your listeners for money.

As unlikely as it might seem, this is a tried-and-true approach among bloggers that has migrated successfully to the world of podcasting. It has the advantage of being relatively straightforward. Your listeners find value in the podcasts you're creating and they compensate you directly for that value. What could be simpler?

There are two basic variations to this approach:

The Tip Jar (or Donation Button)

Podcasters who use the Tip Jar approach simply maintain a link on their websites that allows listeners to make a donation to support the podcast. When a listener clicks on the link, like the one you see in Figure 13.3, they're given the opportunity to make a contribution of any size they want.

FIGURE 13.3

IT Conversations, one of the most well-respected podcasts around, used the Tip Jar approach with a "Donate" link on the top of its web page.

Some podcasters are reluctant to use this model because they feel it is somehow unseemly or unprofessional. The truth is that some of the most well-respected podcasts around use this approach...and some of the biggest bloggers on the Web do, too, for that matter.

If you're going to use a Tip Jar, the easiest way is to set up a PayPal account to accept donations. An existing PayPal account that you might have set up for eBay purchases will do nicely. If you don't have a PayPal account, you can easily set one up at PayPal.com.

The Pledge Drive

This approach, a variation of the Tip Jar model, mimics the pledge drives that you find periodically on public television. With this approach, the normal Tip Jar model is augmented with periodic appeals for contributions.

The Pledge Drive approach has been used successfully in the blogosphere and will likely become a mainstream approach for podcasts over time.

The Sponsorship Model

The third basic model for making money with your podcast is to seek commercial sponsorship. This is, of course, the traditional approach for generating revenue with media of all types: charging a fee for mentioning a sponsor on your podcast. There are different approaches to sponsorship, as we'll discuss in a moment.

Seeking commercial sponsorship has some inherent drawbacks, however, and you'll want to consider them carefully before you decide whether or not it's the right model for you.

Sponsorships Must Be Sold

In a perfect world, you'd answer your phone one afternoon and hear someone on the other end of the line say, "I'm from Vandelay Industries. We just heard about your podcast and think it's terrific. We'd like to sponsor it. How much would that cost?" Like winning the lottery, it would be an exaggeration to say that this *never* happens. It is safe to say, though, that your odds of winning the lottery are only slightly longer than those of having a sponsor seek out your podcast.

In the real world, if you're going to find a sponsor, it's going to be necessary for you to seek out a number of potential sponsors and sell them on the idea of sponsoring your podcast. In all likelihood, you'll have to make several presentations before you're successful. If you're looking for relatively small amounts of money to offset some of your expenses, you'll be able to approach smaller companies with your sales proposition. This is a plausible approach if you have an existing relationship with the decision-makers at a particular company or if your podcast is a particularly good fit for that company's target market.

PODCASTING CAN AUGMENT YOUR OTHER BUSINESS VENTURES

When you think about generating revenue with podcasting, don't overlook the possibility of using your podcast to enhance the value of other business undertakings you might be involved in. One approach would be to use a podcast to provide added value for your existing customers.

An even simpler approach is to use podcasting technology to distribute existing audio content. Many traditional radio shows are being offered via podcast, enhancing their value to advertisers. Similarly, radio host Rush Limbaugh is using podcasting to add to the value of an existing offering for paid subscribers.

Finally, your existing business may deliver presentations from time to time—either to customers or to employees. These presentations can be easily recorded and then distributed with podcasting technology.

The bottom line is that your best business model might not be to make money with your podcasts. It might be to use podcasts to make more money with your other business endeavors.

Larger companies generally allocate their marketing budgets through ad agencies. Selling sponsorships of this sort is a highly competitive undertaking. A sales effort of this sort is time-consuming and can be frustrating, particularly if you're not already adept at selling.

If you decide that this is the right business opportunity for you then it's important to come armed with as much information as possible. The best way to do that is to create a media kit.

Creating a Media Kit

A media kit is simply a concise sales presentation on paper (or in a standard computer file format such as Microsoft Word or Adobe's PDF format) that describes your podcast and its audience. If you're going to be successful offering sponsorships to corporations and their agencies, then an effective media kit, like the one in Figure 13.4, is essential.

FIGURE 13.4

This media kit from the Endurance Radio podcast provides potential sponsors with a concise overview of the podcast and its value proposition.

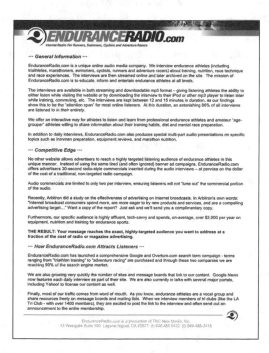

Your media kit should include

- Information about the size of your audience
- Information about the relevant demographic characteristics of your audience
- An overview of what makes your podcast unique
- Specific information about the sponsorship opportunities you're offering, including costs

Your media kit will not sell sponsorships by itself. If you're targeting the corporate market, however, it's a necessary tool for getting the conversation started.

Classic Sponsorship Versus Commercial Placements

By their nature, podcasts are more suited to the type of sponsorship arrangement that calls for a sponsor to underwrite the entire podcast. With this approach, you as the show's host would announce to your listeners something like, "This podcast is being brought to you by our good friends at Vandelay Industries. Let me take a moment to tell you about why you should support Vandelay Industries…"

Commercial placements like those found on traditional radio are generally unsuited to podcasts since listeners can fast forward past them.

The Aggregator Approach to Sponsorship

Another approach to sponsorship that's being developed is the distribution of podcasts through a central directory. The directory, or aggregator, would have the responsibility of attracting listeners. The directory would then sell sponsorships and share some portion of the resulting revenue with the individual podcast producers. Podshow.com is one example of a directory that's trying to develop this business model.

This approach has the advantage of alleviating the need for individual podcasters to sell their own sponsorships. In return, they'd give up control of their financial destinies and would receive only a portion of the revenue that their podcast might otherwise generate. For hobbyist podcasters, this might prove to be an attractive approach if the directory does a good job of generating revenue and attracting listeners.

Distribution to Paid Subscribers

At the beginning of this chapter, we mentioned that there is one way to extract value directly from your podcast's content. That method is to charge listeners to subscribe to your podcast.

As this chapter is being written, there are no examples of this approach to cite. We fully expect, however, that by the time you read this, some podcasters will have begun to offer their shows on a paid subscription basis.

There are two general approaches to doing this. The first involves charging a nominal fee for a subscription and attempting to attract a large audience. The other approach is to charge a large subscription fee to a small, select audience.

As we have said throughout this book, podcasts are not broadcasting. They are generally not designed to attract broad audiences and are not the best vehicle for broad, widespread distribution. That being the case, the prospects for success with a low-cost, high-distribution podcast are questionable. Even so, several companies have indicated that they will be attempting to facilitate such an approach. These companies include

- PayPal (paypal.com)
- BitPass (bitpass.com)
- Click And Buy (clickandbuy.com)
- Javien (javien.com)
- RSS Bazaar (rssbazaar.com)

The second approach strikes us as much more promising if—and this is a big "if"—your podcast contains unique information that's clearly valuable to a specific, well-defined audience. Both approaches will require a sustained marketing effort. Experience in other media demonstrates that selling a $20 subscription takes almost as much effort as selling a $200 subscription. If the content of your podcast lends itself to high-end positioning then this approach is plausible.

Choosing the Right Business Model

In order to be successful at generating revenue from your podcast, it's critical to choose the right business model. As you evaluate your options, take these factors into consideration:

Does it suit your personal skill set and inclinations?

If you've never sold anything in your life and you can't really imagine yourself ever selling anything in the future, then selling sponsorships is not likely to be the right business model for you.

Is it appropriate for the format and content of your podcast?

An affiliate/associate business model is perfect if your podcast naturally references products out in the marketplace. For example, a podcast about podcasting and audio equipment would be well suited to this type of business model. On the other hand, if you're spending most of your podcast telling jokes then the Tip Jar approach might be better for you. (Assuming, of course, that your jokes are actually funny!)

Does it match the requirements of your audience?

A podcast with a corporate audience is probably not going to do well with a Tip Jar approach. That type of audience is not used to that kind of solicitation and is unlikely to be responsive. If you're providing timely technical information that isn't available elsewhere to corporate CIOs, you might get a better response from selling high-end subscriptions.

Other Revenue Opportunities for Podcasters

There's one other type of approach you might want to consider, although it doesn't exactly fall under the heading of generating revenue with your podcast. Our best guess is that corporate America is likely to start turning to podcasting as a mainstream tool for disseminating information to employees and customers. Your skillset as a podcast producer might very well be valuable to corporate clients who want to start podcasting but don't have the in-house expertise.

The economics of podcasting are such that it is going to be attractive to a wide range of companies. With the information in this book under your belt and with a little bit of practice, you'll be able to offer your services to these companies as a podcasting consultant.

THE ABSOLUTE MINIMUM

- If you want to generate revenue with your podcasts, it's critical that you learn as much as you can about your audience.

- Affiliate/associate programs such as the one offered by Amazon are a great way to generate revenue with very little effort while offering value to your listeners at the same time.

- A Tip Jar or Donation Button allows your listeners to contribute to you directly in return for the value they receive from your podcast.

- Selling sponsorships is possible but it is also difficult and can be frustrating for podcasters who aren't inclined toward sales.

- As a podcaster, your skills might be valuable to corporations that want to start podcasting to their employees and customers.

14

MUSIC AND INTELLECTUAL PROPERTY

Every time someone makes a recording (or writes a show note) they create "intellectual property." That property is recognized and protected through a system called copyright. If you're podcasting as a hobby, you might not think you should be worried about copyright, but even if you don't care much about copyright, the people who wrote and recorded the music that you might want to use in your podcast probably do. In this chapter, we'll take a look at copyrights and how to use them—whether they're yours or belong to someone else.

What Is a Copyright?

Copyright is, at the most basic level, exactly what the name implies: the right to make copies of something that has been created. Now, it's important to note that the protection is for the created "thing"—you can't copyright an idea. The copyright of the created "thing" (which the law tends to call an "expression") says that the copyright owner is the one who benefits from sales or performances of the work.

In the U.S., the copyright lasts for the lifetime of the author plus 70 years. If the work is created by a company instead of an individual, the copyright lasts 95 years from its publication or 120 years from its creation, whichever is shorter. Any way you look at it, the law says that you get to benefit from the things you create for a long, long time.

What can you do with a copyright? The same things you can do with anything else you own. You can buy, sell, trade, or transfer copyrights just like you would do with cars or baseball cards. You also get to decide who else can use your property, allowing others to play your podcast—or not. It's your choice.

Now, your copyright comes into existence the moment you create something (such as a podcast). For the copyright to have force in court when it comes to economic damages, though, you have to register your copyright. The United States Library of Congress is the agency that registers copyrights in the U.S., through a process that requires a little time to make a copy of the recording and mail it to the copyright office, and a bit of money (the $25 fee). The process isn't terribly involved, but if you're doing a daily (or even a weekly) podcast, you can see where the fees would start to add up. If you're creating your podcast as a business, then the fee becomes part of your cost of doing business. If it's a hobby, but you still want to have some control over your podcast, then you might consider licensing its use, rather than relying on copyright registration.

> **tip**
>
> The most current, concise information on registering a copyright can be found on the Library of Congress website at http://www.copyright.gov/circs/circ1.html. To register the MP3 file that contains your podcast, you'll want to use form SR (for sound recordings), which can be downloaded from http://www.copyright.gov/forms/formsri.pdf.

Royalties

While you might decide not to register the copyright of your podcast, commercial record producers do register their copyrights, and they expect (and are entitled to) royalties for the recording and public performance of their music. A podcast is, to a great extent, both, and therein lies a problem for the podcaster who wants to include copyrighted music in his or her podcast.

There are royalty structures in place for virtually every type of music recording or performance, with the fees, permissions, and payment methods well defined and understood by those on both ends of the process. Podcasting is so new, and its combination of streaming and recording, storage and transmission, is so filled with possibilities for listening, that the recording industry, government, and the traditional payers of royalties (broadcasting companies and performance producers) haven't yet come to anything like an agreement on how royalties are to be assessed. At the time of this writing, the royalties suggested by the recording industry are a combination of the most expensive licenses available, when they're willing to seriously consider licenses for podcasting music at all. The result is that, if you're looking for a legal way to build a podcast filled with today's popular music, you're out of luck. Unless you are backed by the largest sort of corporation with the deepest sort of pockets, at this writing there simply is no way to license the music that you're likely to hear on popular radio.

There is an exception, but it's very limited; if your podcast is made up of music reviews, and you want to include very brief excerpts of the music you're reviewing, then the use falls under the "incidental use" clause of the copyright and licensing laws (commonly referred to as "fair use"), and you can legally include the music without royalty. There are two keys here; first, you must be reviewing, critiquing, or otherwise discussing the music in question. Next, the music included must be a brief excerpt—you can't include all but the last two seconds of a recording and claim that it's an excerpt. If you want to include full pieces of music in your podcast, you'll need to find music for which you have a license, music that has a license explicitly allowing it to be used in your situation, or music that is released through the Creative Commons—all examples of "podsafe" music you can use.

tip

Getting a definitive word on whether a particular excerpt constitutes "fair use" can be difficult without actually going to trial, and that is a very expensive way to get a legal opinion. If you'd like to see what the Copyright Office has to say on the subject, you can go to http://www.copyright.gov/fls/fl102.html. A more "friendly" explanation can be found at http://fairuse.stanford.edu. The best ideas are to keep excerpts very short, and make sure they're used in the context of a review or critique. If you're making an educational podcast, the rules are slightly different, but only slightly; no matter what your ninth-grade teacher did when copying magazine articles, you can't go around ignoring copyright laws just because you're doing something for an educational purpose.

Podsafe Music for Your Podcast

While many musicians (and their record companies) are concerned about controlling the distribution of music so they can be sure that they're being compensated for each copy, there are other musicians who have other concerns. Some musicians are just getting started, and are much more interested in seeing their music get into as many ears as possible than in denying anyone the ability to download or copy their music. Some musicians get the majority of their income from concert gate revenues, and don't have a record deal, so they see recorded music as a marketing tool to get people into their concerts. Some people just have a view of music performance that includes letting people download or copy their music as much as possible, and donate money as they feel the musician deserves. All of these views (including that of the major record labels) are fine, and there are ways for each group to use copyright and licensing to enforce their particular view. We've already looked at the copyright side of things, so let's spend some time looking at music you can legitimately include in your podcast.

The first type of music people look for is that which carries a no-royalty license. You can find this type of music on CDs of music samples, websites, and on CDs attached to books and magazines. It will explicitly say in the text surrounding the music that it is available for use in any context without a royalty payment. You'll want to be sure that the license covers the type of podcast you're putting together (take special note of whether you're limited to non-commercial use), and you'll need to print out or keep a copy of the license allowing your podcast use just in case there's ever a question from someone who holds (or who believes they hold) the rights to the music.

Next comes music from sites where artists and bands upload their music in hopes of developing an audience and finding a record deal. There are people who will tell you that any music available for downloading from a site such as Garage Band (www.garageband.com) is legal to use in any podcast, but the laws don't support that view. There are some pieces of music that will be available for all uses; others that can be downloaded and listened to, but not used in other recordings; and still others that can be streamed, but not downloaded. Don't assume that a piece of music is podsafe; read the copyright notice and license that accompanies the audio file.

Some artists have their own websites where copies of their performances may be downloaded. By now, you should be getting the picture that music is copyrighted and limited to the most minimal uses unless additional rights are explicitly granted. That's the right picture. The artists will likely have something on their site that explains the rights they're granting—and if you have any doubt, contact the artist. If it's a startup group or artist, they might well allow you to include their music in a podcast, especially if you use a version of the performance that has a voice-over with the artist's name and title of the piece included in the sound file. If the artist refers you to their management or to one of the standard rights agencies then you may have a more serious job ahead of you to get the rights.

There are people who will tell you that a recording isn't copyrighted unless the © symbol, or a certain set of words (like, "Copyright the artist, 2005") is attached to the file. As you saw when we were discussing the copyright to your podcast, the legal rights to any work come into existence when that work is first recorded. It's always safest to assume that any work is distributed under the most restrictive license unless you see something to the contrary explicitly stated.

One of the more interesting new developments in rights statements is the Creative Commons, a system under which copyright holders allow others to use their work without going through a great deal of form-filling and royalty payment. When you're looking for music to include in your podcast, it's good to know that the Creative Commons logo means that you have a very good shot at being able to use the music in your podcast.

FIGURE 14.1

"Some Rights Reserved" means that the author allows you to use the work through the terms of the Creative Commons license.

There are several standard Creative Commons licenses. Each comes with three components: a logo that is attached to the file and hosting website, an easily human-readable version, and the full legal text. You're most likely to see one of three versions of the Creative Commons license (out of six possibilities).

- **Attribution** is the most liberal option. As long as you give proper credit to the author, you can use the work in just about any way you want, even if you include it in a commercial podcast.

- **Attribution Share-Alike** allows you to use the work as you wish as long as you give proper credit to the author and license your resulting work under the same terms—an important limitation if your podcast is commercial.

- **Attribution Non-Commercial** says that you can use the work in any way you want, as long as you give proper credit to the author, with the exception of commercial work—in other words, you can't make money off of the license-holder's work.

FIGURE 14.2

The symbols for three Creative Commons licenses: Attribution, Attribution Share-Alike, and Attribution Non-Commercial.

 Attribution Non-Commercial

 Attribution Share-Alike

Attribution

The Creative Commons is a way for authors to allow their work to spread while maintaining some control over its use. It's very exciting to see the use of Creative Commons licenses when you're looking for works to include in your podcast.

Fair Use

What if you take a recorder to a concert and capture the performance for inclusion in your podcast? You'd own the rights to that, wouldn't you? The answer is "probably not," unless you are also the songwriter and performer for the performance in question. Copyright law recognizes the rights of the author and of the performer, and both must be secured before a performance is recorded and distributed. These dual rights are why, for example, school musical performances so often carry an order against recording from the audience—the school has been granted a license by the author (or the publisher, acting for the author) to publicly perform the piece, but not to record it. You should know that you have the permission of everyone who holds copyright to the music being performed before you set up to record and podcast a performance.

So what is this "fair use" that people like to talk about? In most cases, it's the sort of thing we discussed in the first part of this chapter; there are three broad circumstances when you can use *part* of someone's work within your own. First, if your podcast is a review or critique of a recording, you can use short excerpts to illustrate your point. For example, if you loved the guitar solo on a particular song, you could play a few seconds of the solo to let your audience share in your excitement. Next, if you're teaching some point about the music, you can use a short

tip

Satire and Parody—is there a difference? There sure is. Parody is a work that imitates an artist's style in a humorous way. Satire is a work that holds some of society's failings or foibles up to the light. Parodies must be based, to some extent, on existing works, while satires are often completely original. Parody is explicitly protected under copyright law.

excerpt to illustrate a teaching point. If, to continue the example, the guitar solo was performed in Mixolydian mode, you might play a few seconds of the solo during a lecture on "The Use of Mixolydian Mode in Popular Music."

The third major category for "fair use" comes into play when you want to make a parody based on an existing piece. If you want to make a podcast that uses song parodies to comment on the state of music, politics, or the silliness of the world at large, copyright law allows you to do so. The key here is to make sure that it's obvious you're creating a parody; merely adding your own words to a famous melody doesn't pass the test. Note that this is the only category of fair use that allows you access to the entire length of a piece, though most parodies use only the melody or, less commonly, only the lyrics, with the parody coming through pairing the well-known component with devastatingly witty new ingredients.

Resources for Understanding Royalties and Copyrights

Understanding how copyright laws apply to music and how it's used in broadcasting, film, and the Internet can be complicated, but there are a number of websites available to help explain the details of getting the rights to a piece of music for your podcast.

- **The Harry Fox Agency**

  http://www.harryfox.com/index.jsp

  The Harry Fox Agency is the organization that the vast majority of commercial music copyright holders use to administer the "mechanical rights" to their intellectual property. Mechanical rights are the rights to use an existing recording. If you hear popular music in a film or television program, the odds are very good that the rights were negotiated through, and administered by, the Harry Fox Agency. The website includes a great deal of information on standard licensing rates, the procedures to follow to request a license, and what you should expect as you move through the process.

- **BMI**

  http://www.bmi.com

  Broadcast Music International (BMI) is an organization that collects license fees for public broadcast performances—including radio, television, and Internet airplay—on behalf of composers, publishers, or their agents. BMI is one of the key organizations involved in figuring out how the royalty structure for music in podcasts will work. Check their website for details of the current state of royalty payments, and to listen to the BMI podcast of new songwriters.

ASCAP

http://www.ascap.org

The American Society of Composers, Authors and Publishers (ASCAP) is the organization that collects royalties for the public, non-dramatic performance of a work. When a concert takes place, ASCAP is the organization that takes care of collecting the royalties on behalf of the songwriters. Since many performances are recorded for later distribution, ASCAP becomes involved for the public performance piece of the royalty puzzle.

RIAA

http://www.riaa.com

The Recording Industry Association of America is the trade group made up of record producers and distributors. Since most people listen to music via recordings, the RIAA cares deeply about making sure that the recordings heard are legitimate. The RIAA is one of the groups that has expressed grave concerns about the effects of podcasting on artists, and is a key to any industrywide agreement on the royalty structure for podcasts involving music.

SoundExchange

http://www.soundexchange.com

While the organizations listed so far deal with the rights and royalties for the composers or songwriters, SoundExchange is concerned with collecting royalties for the performers. Like BMI and ASCAP, SoundExchange is a central collection organization for performers, allowing those who broadcast recordings to have a single agency to deal with. The SoundExchange website has a ton of information on the state of performer royalties.

SESAC

www.sesac.com

SESAC does the same sort of thing that BMI and ASCAP do; it simply represents a different group of songwriters and composers. SESAC is smaller than either BMI or ASCAP, but may well be the representative for the composer you're interested in. Look at the website to see the approach that SESAC takes to figuring out how many times a particular piece of music has been played, and thus the amount of the royalty to be paid.

How Do Royalties and Music Publishing Work?

http://www.bugmusic.com/frontdoor/faq.cfm

Bug Music is another agency that administers royalties and licenses for copyright holders. This FAQ page has a great set of explanations of the terms and procedures you'll be using when you go to license music for a project. The language is simple and easy to understand even if the application of some concepts (number of listeners for an online program, for example) isn't.

■ **Public Domain Music**

http://www.pdinfo.com/

The definition of public domain music is fairly simple: It's music for which the copyright has expired, or for which the copyright owner has explicitly given ownership of the rights to "the public" at large. The practical impact is that you won't have to pay royalties to use public domain since there's no one to whom you can pay the fee. How do you know whether a piece of music is in the public domain? Going to this site is a good way to begin to answer that question. This site has lists of pieces that are in the public domain, as well as sound files of recordings that have passed into the public domain.

Links to Royalty-Free Music

Don't confuse royalty-free music with music for which there is no fee for use—music in the public domain, or which has been released under Creative Commons licenses. Instead, royalty-free music is music for which you pay a single, flat fee for the right to distribute or broadcast. Royalty-free music can be a super solution if you want a piece to use as a theme song for all your podcasts, or if you want a certain "feeling" at a particular point in all your podcasts. For a single fee, you license a piece for inclusion in multiple shows, and distribution in any format.

There are many publishers who specialize in royalty-free music; the three listed here are three possibilities, not the only three options that exist.

■ http://www.loopmasters.com/copyright_free_music_royalty_free_music_
   links.htm

■ http://www.flyinghands.com/

■ http://www.studio1productions.com/

THE ABSOLUTE MINIMUM

Copyright is the legal right to control and profit from something you've created. You don't have to do anything special to own the copyright—it's created automatically as soon as you've created the work.

If you want to be able to defend your copyright in court, you'll need to register your copyright with the Library of Congress. For podcasts, form SR is the proper form to use, and a copy can be downloaded from the Library of Congress website.

If you want to retain some control over how your intellectual property is used, you may release it under the terms of the Creative Commons. This system, based upon

continues

the GNU Public License frequently used by software authors, doesn't require a fee for the license to use a work, but may place certain limitations on the person using the material.

Under certain very special conditions you may use portions of a copyrighted work without asking permission of the copyright holder. If you're writing a critique or teaching a class, you can use short excerpts from a piece to illustrate a particular point, but you may not include the entire piece in your class or podcast. If you're writing a parody of a particular song, you may use the melody, for example, though the words you put with it must be different from the original, and must be a parody of the original work.

If you're interested in learning more about the process of licensing music, there are websites, such as the sites for the Harry Fox Agency and Bug Music, that have pages where you can read in considerably more depth about the topics.

15

Protecting Your Content Through Packaging

The question of protecting your content—making sure that your podcast is recognized as your work and not ripped-off by others—can often be settled by making the podcast uniquely yours. The methods we'll cover come down to building a solid website around the podcast, illustrating your podcast with images, and looking beyond the basic RSS feed for distributing your podcast. We've already talked about developing your podcast personality and creating content that couldn't come from anyone else. Now, let's take just a few minutes to talk about ways to wrap your podcast in supporting material that adds to the podcast's enjoyment and value while keeping it yours alone.

Wrapping Your Podcast in a Good Website

Here's a startling revelation: Most podcasts are about something. That something can be your business, your cat, your vacation, or your love life, but most podcasts aren't random ramblings on disjointed topics. We bring this up because there's a good chance that someone else has created a podcast, or a blog, or a website on a similar topic, and it's easy to link to those resources on the website that carries your podcast. While it's true that those links can lead people away from your site, the Internet tends to be an interlinked place, so through trackback links and invitation, many of the related sites will include your podcast on their list of related sites, so their visitors can find you. The readers win, you win, and your increasingly rich set of links and resources become part of the total on-line experience that makes your podcast unique.

Of course, one of the important things many podcasters do is blog about their podcasts. Within a blog, it's easy to set up the expectations for the podcast, or to talk about the circumstances surrounding the actual podcasting process. If you decided to turn on comments for your blog, it also makes a great way for your podcast listeners to get you feedback—to make the entire podcasting experience more interactive and richer for both you and your listeners.

> **tip**
>
> Trackback is a standard created by the team that wrote Moveable Type, one of the first blog software programs. Creating a trackback link is very easy using most blog software. For a full explanation of how and why it works, visit http://www.movabletype.org/ trackback/beginners/.

FIGURE 15.1

Podcast transcripts and location photos can make the website more inviting.

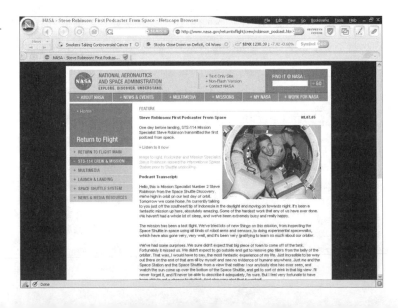

Podcasts with Pictures

We first talked about photos to accompany podcasts in the section on recording in the field and "sound seeing" at the end of Chapter 7, "Recording Your Podcast." Beyond the obvious technique of showing the location the audience will be hearing, photos can help personalize your podcast in other ways.

First, think about the possibilities of using ID3 tags to include a photo of yourself, or of a podcast mascot, that appears on the screen of the MP3 player each time your podcast is played. Associating sound with a photo or image can help "brand" the podcast, making it much more difficult for anyone else to claim it for their own without raising a red flag among the listeners.

FIGURE 15.2

Photographs of podcast participants can help make the listener feel closer to the artist.

Next, consider adding photos and even short video clips to the website as a way of making the total experience richer. Figure 15.2 shows a podcast page where the artists featured on the podcast are shown along with the show notes. (Note: While we've talked about the difficulty of getting the rights to music for a podcast, the podcast shown on this screenshot is one of the licensing bodies—they are able to give themselves permission with little difficulty.) Listeners with photo-capable MP3 players will be able to download photos to view while listening to your podcast, and those without that capability can still look at the images and clips, either before or after listening to the podcast, to gain a deeper sense of what you're doing. On the whole, though, remember that listening to a podcast is an essentially portable, mobile experience, so be careful about doing anything that depends on the listener being tied to the Internet or their computer while listening to the podcast.

Alternate Packaging—Passwords and More

If you are podcasting as a hobby or as part of a startup business then distributing your podcast through a website or an RSS feed will define your options. These aren't by any means bad options, and they will be the choices of the overwhelming majority of podcasters and their listeners.

One option often asked about is password protecting an RSS feed. It's possible to do this, but it's not particularly easy, and many of the RSS aggregators don't handle passwords with any grace. It's much easier to password-protect your site (or particular pages from your site) to place limits on the people who can reach the XML button to begin with. If you're not an expert in web scripting, you should get someone's pre-written scripts to use. One option is to build your site, with the blog features for your show notes and management of all your content using scripts from http://www.newsscript.co.uk/. The Xtra version of the software costs $19 and has scripts that convert HTML code into RSS feeds, making one less thing that you have to worry about. NewsScript is a complete content management system that includes password protection among its features.

Another possibility for corporate-sponsored podcasts is distribution on USB flash memory drives. These small devices can be purchased for low cost in bulk, and for small memory sizes, and make superb transport mechanisms for MP3 files. Easily branded with corporate identity information, they are easy to use in bulk recording devices for distributing podcasts to lots of people in a very controlled fashion.

THE ABSOLUTE MINIMUM

In the final analysis, nothing protects your work as well as developing a distinctive style and unique content for your podcasts.

- Think about making the website that carries your podcast a richer experience
- Use ID3 tags and simple photos to marry an image to your podcast for listeners who have a photo-enabled MP3 player
- Don't spend too much time worrying about passwords for your RSS feed—they will break too many readers
- If distribution control concerns your business, think about USB memory drives as a means to carry your podcast

16

Letting Your Podcast Go—Taking a Wider View of Rights

After all the talk about how to protect your intellectual property rights, and the importance of respecting the rights of others, it might seem odd to see a chapter on letting your podcast go. For many podcasters, though, letting go will be the best approach to intellectual property rights. If you're not trying to make money with your podcast, or if your business model depends on having as many people as possible hear your podcast, then trying to limit access in any way can be self-defeating. With the current state of podcasting, spreading the word can be more important than the details of claiming ownership and rights. Even within the realm of letting go, though, there are degrees of rights claimed and granted, and it's worth thinking about the costs and benefits of ignoring the whole situation, the open source model, and taking advantage of Creative Commons.

Maybe You Can Just Let Go

Ignoring the whole rights issue has a certain elegant simplicity, and for podcasts to which no financial value is assigned, this simplicity makes a world of sense. You're not going to sue anyone over your podcast anyway, and there are no symbols or phrases attached to the podcast that might frighten people from reproducing and sharing your podcast, or from using your podcast in some sort of mashup that takes on its own life. The best part of this approach is that you have to do absolutely nothing to take advantage of its non-existent protections. Create your podcast, send it out into the world, and enjoy the fact that you've contributed to the intellectual life of the planet.

If you want to formalize the "letting go," you can place your podcast in the public domain. When you place something in the public domain, you're making a statement renouncing all private rights to it. That means others can copy or use it, because it belongs to everyone—and no one. The nice thing is that you can place something in the public domain through a simple declaration, with no special forms, complicated licenses, or government agencies involved. It's important to remember, though, that it's a one-way street; once you place something in the public domain, you can't go back and re-assert your rights later. If you want to keep some control over the podcast (even if it's just making sure that you're acknowledged as the author), then there are other possibilities you should explore.

If you don't want to sell your podcast (or anything attached to it), but you would like to be recognized for your creation, there are a couple of options available to you. The first is to license listeners based on the open-source software model. This means, in essence, creating a license that says people may listen to your podcast and share it as long as they give you credit. Most open-source licenses would also let people make mashups or mixes of your podcast as long as their product was distributed with the same sort of open-source license. Now, you should understand that the open-source model was designed for software, not content, and may not be a perfect fit. For a license that owes much to the open-source model but may be a better fit for your podcast, you should look to Creative Commons for a variety of options that might well work for you.

> **tip**
>
> To see the open-source license and how it might apply to you and your podcast, go to www.opensource.org. You'll find a copy of several licenses and boilerplate text you can include on your website to accompany your podcast. The most common free software license, the GNU Public License (GPL), can be found, along with a great deal of documentation on the philosophy behind the free software movement, at www.gnu.org.

Creative Commons

Creative Commons started in 2001 as a project to take some of the ideas of the open-source movement, especially the GNU Project, and apply them to content. Where many commercial audio and video productions bear the words, "All Rights Reserved," Creative Commons is based on the concept of Some Rights Reserved. Now, Creative Commons has licenses specifically designed for books, movies, video, and other content forms, but you'll be most interested in the licenses designed for audio recordings. There are four different categories of license, each granting a different set of uses. They are

- Attribution
- Non-commercial
- No Derivative Works
- Share Alike

Attribution allows downloaders to listen to your podcast, copy it, distribute it, and create derivative works based on it, but only if they give you proper credit.

Non-commercial says that your podcast listeners can listen to, copy, distribute, and create derivative works based on your podcast, but only if they're doing it as a hobby or for school work—they're not allowed to try to make money off of your podcast.

No Derivative Works allows your listeners to listen to and distribute your podcast, but doesn't allow them to create anything that derives from your work—no mashups, for example, or long show compilations that include your podcast.

> **tip**
>
> On the Creative Commons web site (www.creativecommons.org) there are ID3 tags you can insert into your podcast's MP3 file, text to insert into your RSS feed's XML file, and code to add to your website or blog's metadata to make sure that all your listeners are aware of the license you're granting to your works, no matter how they obtain the file. Plan to take advantage of all these, and use the Creative Commons logo on your website, to let listeners know how you feel about the issue of your intellectual property rights.

Finally, Share Alike means that listeners can create derivative works from yours, but only if their work is then distributed under a license similar to yours. This license is the one most like the GNU license that is commonly used by people writing computer software.

When you look through the licenses available from Creative Commons, you will likely find one that exactly matches the way you want to express your rights to your podcast. If you have any doubts, the Creative Commons website, www.creativecommons.org, has a series of questions that, when answered, help you choose the appropriate license. Once that's done, you're shown text and an icon to place on your website and in your media, and your work is protected by the license.

THE ABSOLUTE MINIMUM

Your podcast is your intellectual property from the moment you create it. While it's possible to strenuously protect those rights, sometimes it's better to take a more expansive view of the rights situation. While it's possible to produce a podcast that doesn't carry any rights information at all, Creative Commons makes it easy to let people listen to, distribute, and even use your podcast as part of other creative works while still giving you credit, and allowing you some control over its use. Creative Commons licenses are easy, free, and show that you do take your creative work seriously.

- You own the copyright to what you create, so you aren't required to do anything else to have legal ownership of your work.

- Creative Commons licenses are available for a variety of rights and uses.

- The Creative Commons website (www.creativecommons.org) has tools to help you decide which license to use.

- Once you've decided on a license, you can add text to your website or blog, ID3 tags to your podcast's MP3 files, and text to the XML code for the RSS feed to remind your listeners of how they can use your podcast.

PART V

APPENDICES

Glossary

Knowing these terms will help you sound like a veteran podcaster.

AAC   Stands for *Advanced Audio Coding*, this is the audio file format that is used by Apple Computers in its iTunes Music Store. Based on the MPEG-4 standard (a newer, more advanced standard than MP3), AAC files are generally considered to sound somewhat better than MP3 files compressed at a comparable (or even higher) bit rate. Most music players other than iPods do not support the AAC file format.

Aggregator   Specialized software that detects and reads RSS feeds. Specialized aggregators designed to locate and download podcasts are referred to as *iPodders* or *podcatching software*. These aggregators allow you to subscribe to those podcasts that interest you. They will then automatically download new episodes of those podcasts when they become available and, optionally, synchronize them with your music jukebox software and/or your portable music player.

Attachment   See *enclosure*.

Bandwidth   The data capacity of a connection between computers. While the term is usually used to describe the size of the "data pipe" between machines (that is, the amount of data that can be transmitted in a fixed amount of time), it is also used to describe the amount of data that moves through an online web account in a given period of time. It's significant to podcasters because web hosting accounts often set limits for bandwidth and charge for any excess bandwidth that's used.

Bitrate   The amount of data (measured in bits) that's created by one second of audio in an MP3 file. A higher bitrate yields better sound quality but creates larger files.

Blog   A journal that is created and managed online. Podcasts often have accompanying blogs that are used by podcasters as a vehicle for disseminating their show notes.

Compression   An audio effect that makes the volume of an audio track more uniform, reducing the disparity between the track's loudest points and its softest points. In general, compression enhances the listenability of your podcast, particularly for listeners who are using low-quality earbuds or speakers.

Compression is also used to refer to the process by which an audio file is translated into a format that preserves most (but not all) of the file's audio information while producing a file that is significantly smaller in size than the original. MP3 and AAC are both compressed file formats.

Copyright   Specific legal protections that are provided to the owners and creators of intellectual property.

Creative Commons   A not-for-profit organization that offers a flexible, less-restrictive alternative to artists instead of traditional copyright protection mechanisms. Information about the organization and terms of the Creative Commons license can be found at creativecommons.org.

Decibel   A measure of the difference in loudness as the volume of a signal is adjusted. In general, one decibel is the smallest difference that a listener can perceive while a 10 decibel increase effectively doubles a signal's loudness.

Digital Rights Management   Technology that allows a content provider to limit access to digital content. For example, Digital Right Management prevents someone from distributing music they've purchased in the iTunes music store.

Double-Ender   A technique for creating a podcast from two separately recorded audio sources. Typically, two individuals will have a conversation with each one recording his own part. Editing software then allows the two recordings to be stitched together into a single audio file that sounds as if the two parts were recorded together.

Enclosure   A file that is attached to an electronic communication. Most computer users are familiar with this concept as it's applied to email, where it's often referred to as an *attachment*. Podcasts can be delivered as enclosures or attachments to an RSS feed.

Encoding   The process of translating raw audio information into a particular file format.

Feed   Another name for an RSS file. Your podcatching (aggregator) software checks the feed to see if there's new content available on your website.

File Format   The way a computer file is structured so that its information can be understood by other computers or devices such as portable music players. There are several file formats for audio information including MP3 and AAC. While information can often be translated easily from one format to another, formats are not usually compatible with one another. A portable music player that understands the MP3 format, for example, will often not be able to work with files in AAC format.

FTP   An acronym for *File Transfer Protocol*. This is the technology most often used to move large files from one location to another. Typically, you'll use FTP to send your podcast up to your web host's server.

Headset   A set of headphones combined with a microphone in a single unit. One advantage of using a headset is that is maintains a uniform distance between your mouth and the microphone. Many podcasters find headsets to be more convenient than using a separate mic and headphones.

ID3 Tag   Specially formatted information that is attached to an MP3 file. On an audio file that contains a song, the ID3 tag will specify the song's title, the album from which it came, the artist's name, the song's genre, and the year in which it was released. Podcasters use ID3 tags to append information about a podcast to the file in which it's delivered. The results can be less than satisfactory, though, since the ID3 specification was created specifically for information about music, not podcasts.

iPodder   Originally, iPodder referred to the specific podcatching software package that was available on iPodder.org. The term has become somewhat generic over time and is now often used to refer to any aggregator software for podcasts. (See *aggregator*.)

Licensing   The legal arrangement under which music can be used. Licensing defines the conditions under which a particular piece of music can be played as well as the royalty payment due to the composer and artist. (See *Podsafe music*.)

Loop   A short audio segment that is repeated multiple times. Loops are the building block of much of the music that's generated with Apple's GarageBand software.

Mastering   Following the mixing process, this is the process of creating the final edited, mixed track that will be your podcast. This is the last step in the podcast creating process before encoding.

Mixing   The process of using audio recording software to put two or more tracks together, aligning the tracks and adjusting the relative volume levels appropriately. For example, it is during the mixing process that you might lower the volume of a music track so that a voice track playing simultaneously can be heard clearly.

MP3   One of several popular file formats for audio files. MP3 files are the current industry standard for audio files, in general, and podcasts, in particular.

Podcast   A radio-like show that is recorded to an MP3 file and then distributed over the Internet. A distinctive feature of podcasts is that they are made available for distribution as an enclosure to an RSS feed. Listeners can download the file and listen to it on a portable music player or they can listen to it as an audio stream on their computers.

Podcatching Software   See *aggregator*.

Podsafe Music   Music that is made available for use in podcasts by the artists and composers without standard royalty obligations. Artists who provide podsafe music usually do so in return for exposure that isn't available to them through commercial broadcast outlets.

Promo   A short audio commercial for a particular podcast, usually produced by the producer of that podcast and then played on other podcasts.

RSS (Really Simple Syndication)   A technology that allows interested individuals to automatically monitor your website for new content. This is the technology that automatically delivers your podcasts to listeners who have "subscribed" to your podcast. The RSS feed announces that a new podcast is available and makes the podcast accessible as an enclosure.

Sample Rate   The number of times per second that audio software takes a "snapshot" of an analog audio signal as it converts that analog information to a digital format. A higher sample rate (more snapshots per second) provides higher quality digital audio but also results in a larger file.

Show Notes   Additional information about topics referenced in your podcast that you make available on the Web for your listeners. Most often, this consists of links to websites mentioned in your podcast. Also, show notes often contain links to photos of people, places, or things that were mentioned on your show.

Signal   Any audio information that registers on your audio recording software. In podcasting, this term will usually refer to a voice signal that is generated by speaking into a microphone.

Skype   A service that provides free high-quality VoIP calling between its users. For a nominal fee, it also allows you to make calls into the traditional phone network.

Sound-Seeing   The audio equivalent of sight-seeing, sound-seeing consists of verbally describing an environment for your podcast audience. Father Roderick Vonhögen's sound-seeing tours of the Vatican on his Catholic Insider podcast are a terrific example of this genre.

Streaming Audio   Audio that is played over your computer but not actually down-loaded to your hard drive. Even though pod-cast listeners often stream a podcast's audio rather than downloading it, music licensing organizations consider podcasts to be down-loads and, therefore, subject to a different licensing structure that is cost-prohibitive.

Sweeper   A very short audio clip that identi-fies you and/or your podcast. Sweepers are often used to segue between segments of your show, especially before or after music.

Track   A discrete segment of recorded audio. While some podcasts consist of a single recorded track, a typical podcast will usually consist of several tracks mixed together. Most recording software will accommodate multiple audio tracks and will allow you to edit each track separately before mixing them together.

VoIP   An acronym that stands for *Voice over IP* (Internet Protocol), this term refers to the technology that allows users to make phone calls over the Internet rather than over tradi-tional phone lines. VoIP technology is impor-tant to podcasters because it allows you to record conversations more easily and with higher quality than would be possible over phone lines.

Web Hosting   The service provided by a company that maintains a presence for your website and/or podcast on the Internet. Web hosting companies typically charge according to the amount of data you store on their servers and the amount of bandwidth (data transfer) you use. Large podcasts take up more space and consume more bandwidth than smaller ones, something you'll want to con-sider as your podcast gains popularity.

XML   An acronym for Extensible Markup Language, XML allows web application designers to create their own customized tags for web documents. For podcasters, it is the technology that facilitates RSS and allows aggregator software to find podcasts on the Internet.

RESOURCES FOR PODCASTERS

There's no shortage of resources available—both online and offline—to support your podcasting efforts. The companies and websites listed here offer all of the software, equipment, and services you'll need to successfully create, post, and syndicate your podcast.

Audio Software for Podcasters

Whether you're creating a simple audio blog or something more elaborate, you'll need software that allows you to capture or record any sound on your computer, then mix and edit it into a podcast. The companies listed here provide audio software for every level of functionality and every computer platform.

Audacity
audacity.sourceforge.net

LineIn
www.rogueamoeba.com

Bias Peak
www.bias-inc.com

MegaSeg
www.megaseg.com

CastBlaster
www.castblaster.com

MixCast Live
www.mixcastlive.com

DSP Quattro
www.i3net.it

Podcast Wizard
www.podcastwizard.com

GarageBand
www.apple.com/garageband

Propaganda
www.makepropaganda.com

Industrial Audio
www.IndustrialAudioSoftware.com

Sound Studio
www.felttip.com

Pod-catching (Aggregator) Software

These companies provide software and/or services for subscribing to podcasts.

Blog Matrix
www.blogmatrix.com

iPodderX
ipodderx.com

Doppler Radio
www.dopplerradio.net

iTunes
www.apple.com/itunes

iPod Agent
www.ipodsoft.com

JPodder
www.jpodder.com

iPodder
ipodder.sourceforge.net

Nimiq
www.nimiq.nl

PodFeeder
www.podfeeder.com

RSSRadio
www.dorada.co.uk

Audio Equipment Manufacturers

When you're ready to take the quality of your podcasts beyond what the built-in mic on your computer can handle, you'll need specialized audio equipment. The companies in this section manufacture gear—from microphones to mixers—that can meet even your most stringent requirements.

AKG
www.akg.com

Peavey
www.peavey.com

Alesis
www.alesis.com

Pioneer
www.pioneerelectronics.com

American Audio
www.americanaudio.us

Samson
www.samsontech.com

Behringer
www.behringer.com

M-Audio
www.m-audio.com

Creative Technology
www.creative.com

Sennheiser
www.sennheiserusa.com

dbx
www.dbxpro.com

Shure
www.shure.com

Electro Voice
www.electrovoice.com

Stanton
www.stantondj.com

e-Mu
www.emu.com

Tascam
www.tascam.com

Korg
www.korg.com

Vestax
www.vestax.com

Mackie
www.mackie.com

Yamaha
http://www.yamaha.com/proaudio/home/

Numark
www.numark.com

Podcasting Directories

You'll make it easier for prospective listeners to find your podcast if you're listed in as many podcasting directories as possible. Here are some of the most popular and important podcasting directories around.

Cast Register
www.castregister.com

Podcast.net
www.podcast.net

Digital Podcast
www.digitalpodcast.com

Podcast411
www.podcast411.com

iPodder
ipodder.org

Podcast Alley
www.podcastalley.com

iPodderX
ipodderx.com/directory

Podcast Directory
www.podcastdirectory.com

Odeo
www.odeo.com

Pod Feed
www.podfeed.net

Open Media Network
www.omn.org

PodShow.com
www.podshow.com

Penguin Radio
www.penguinradio.com/podcasting

Public Radio Fan
www.publicradiofan.com

Online Resources for Podcasters

These companies provide royalty-free music, sound effects, and other services that can make your podcast easier to create or more entertaining to listen to.

AudioBlog
www.audioblog.com

Royalty Free Music
www.RoyaltyFreeMusic.com

Blog Matrix
www.blogmatrix.com

Shockwave-Sound.com
www.shockwave-sound.com

The Free Sound Project
http://freesound.iua.upf.edu/

StockMusic.net
www.stockmusic.net

Online Suppliers of Audio Equipment

When it's time to buy audio equipment, here are some of the best online stores we've found.

American Musical
anandtech.dealtime.com/
xCH-computers

BSW
www.bswusa.com/podcast.asp

Industrial Audio
www.IndustrialAudioSoftware.com

Musician's Friend
www.musiciansfriend.com

Sam Ash
www.samash.com

Sweetwater
www.sweetwater.com

The Podcasting Community Online

As the number of podcasters has grown, a number of online "meeting and greeting" places have appeared that can facilitate your connecting with other podcasters. Whatever problems or questions you might have, chances are that someone has been there before you. These websites will allow you to connect with other podcasters, to share ideas and information, and to find out what's going on in the world of podcasting.

Engadget
www.engadget.com

Podcast and Portable Media Expo
www.portablemediaexpo.com

Podcast Alley
www.podcastalley.com

Podcast Expert
www.podcastexpert.com

Podcast Rigs
www.podcastrigs.com

Podcasting News
www.podcastingnews.com

Ultimate Podcasting
www.ultimatepodcasting.com

Web Hosting and RSS Feed Software and Services

Some podcasters choose to post their podcasts and then syndicate them from their own websites. Other podcasters, however, take advantage of websites and services that streamline all or part of the podcasting process. These companies offer the support services you'll need if you're not inclined to do it all yourself.

Feed Burner
www.feedburner.com

Feeder
www.reinventedsoftware.com

Feed For All
www.feedforall.com

Liberated Syndication
www.libsyn.com

Radio Userland
radio.userland.com

RSS Bazaar
www.rssbazaar.com

C

30 Podcasts You Should Definitely Check Out

One of the most wonderful things about the podcasting community is the incredibly wide range of interests it accommodates. This diverse collection of podcasts will give you a sense of what's out there and will, we're sure, give you plenty of ideas for what to do with your own podcast.

The Daily Source Code

http://live.curry.com/rss.xml

If you want to get the zeitgeist of today's podcasting community, Adam Curry's podcast is de rigueur. As a podcaster, Curry is fearless and occasionally outrageous, working without a safety net and putting the results on display for all to see. Sure, there's an occasional "splat," but for the most part it's entertaining.

WGBH Morning Stories Podcast

http://streams.wgbh.org/podcast/morningstories.xml

Repurposed content from Boston's PBS radio station. Smart stories, superior production values, and a progressive sensibility.

The Point Podcast

http://pfiggianimsc.com/blog/rss.xml

One of the premier podcasts about podcasting, this show features audio guru Paul Figgiani talking about the latest podcasting gear and software in his signature New York style.

New York Minute

http://feeds.feedburner.com/PodcastNYC-NewYorkMinute

Everything you need to know about getting around in The Big Apple, with a little bit of New York history thrown in at no extra charge. The New York Minute podcast is a terrific resource for information about dining, entertainment, sightseeing, and just about anything else you'd want to know about New York City.

Ultimate Podcasting

http://www.ultimatepodcasting.com/UltimatePodcasting.xml

You can file this one under the heading of "Shameless Plugs." This is the companion podcast to *The Absolute Beginner's Guide to Podcasting*. It began while the book was in process, first counting down the days until the manuscript was finished, then counting down the days until publication. Now, it features George's and Curt's observations on the news and trends in the world of podcasting.

Reel Reviews

http://realreviewsradio.com/podcast.xml

Podcasting pioneer Michael Geoghegan shares his thoughts on an idiosyncratic collection of new and classic movies.

The Cubicle Escape Pod

http://feeds.feedburner.com/cubicleescape

Advice for would-be entrepreneurs from a couple of guys who have been there, done that, and are in the process of doing it all over again. Once and future entrepreneurs Jonathan Brown and Matt Thompson talk about what it takes in the real world to get a new business up and running.

The Dawn and Drew Show

http://www.dawnanddrew.com/rss2.xml

A twenty-something married couple from Wisconsin talking about anything and everything that comes to mind. (And when we say "everything," we mean *everything*. This may be the only podcast out there where even the show's phone number is not suitable for publication in this book!) Not for everyone, but consistently one of the most popular podcasts on Podcast Alley. Be aware before you listen that this show has a decidedly adult tone.

Science @ NASA

http://science.nasa.gov/podcast.xml

If science fiction isn't hardcore enough for you, how about some real science? This is the official podcast from the National Aeronautics and Space Administration. If you like science and space then it doesn't get any better than this.

Inside Mac Radio

http://www.osxfaq.com/rss/radio.xml

Repurposed radio content that discusses all things Macintosh (with a liberal dose of iPod information thrown in for good measure). Terrific information about hardware, software, peripherals, and accessories if you're a Mac user, but you can probably pass on this one if you're not.

The President's Weekly Radio Address

http://feeds.feedburner.com/PresidentialWeeklyRadioAddress

Chances are, you've been hearing references in news stories for years about something or other the President said in his weekly radio address but you've probably never actually heard one of the addresses. This is your chance to fix that.

One America Committee

http://www.oneamericacommittee.com/podcast.xml

A podcast from 2004 vice-presidential candidate John Edwards. You don't think he might be getting ready to run again, do you?

Off The Record

http://www.gop.com/PodCast/PodCast.xml

One of a few podcasts launched by the GOP, this particular podcast is a series of interviews with Republican movers and shakers.

Catholic Insider

http://feeds.feedburner.com/catholicinsider

This podcast is hosted by Father Roderick Vonhögen, a Catholic priest based in the Netherlands. Father Vonhögen conducts interviews, gives soundseeing tours, and provides commentary on topics related to the church.

Slice of Sci-Fi

http://sliceofscifi.com/podcast.xml

For the past generation, many of the early adopters of almost every new technology have been science fiction aficionados. Podcasting has proven to be no exception. Michael Mennenga and Evo Terra use their podcast to keep listeners up-to-date on all things sci-fi.

IT Conversations

http://feeds.feedburner.com/ITConversations-EverythingMP3

Doug Kaye's podcast about information technology issues is notable for two reasons. The first is the high quality of the content. The other reason is that Kaye has created what is, in effect, the first "open source" podcast, enlisting the support of listeners—not only financial support but editing, developing, and engineering support as well.

Geek News Central

http://www.geeknewscentral.com/podcast.xml

The name says it all. This is a podcast by geeks and for geeks. If you're not sure whether it's for you, it very well might not be. On the other hand, if your everyday conversations are littered with three letter abbreviations then this might be the regular tech fix you crave.

Caribbean Free Radio

http://feeds.feedburner.com/CaribbeanFreeRadioBlog

Georgis Popplewell's podcast from Trinidad and Tobago about all things Caribbean including regular updates on the escapades of Delphine, a headstrong Caribbean mongrel!

The Podcast Brothers

http://feeds.feedburner.com/PodcastBrothers

This a podcast is about making money with podcasting. Even if your podcast is primarily a labor of love—which is the case with the vast majority of podcasts—Tim and Emile Bourquin still have idea you can easily implement to offset some of your expenses.

Endurance Radio

http://feeds.feedburner.com/EnduranceRadioDailyAudioInterview

This podcast by Tim Bourquin was created for runners, cyclists, swimmers, and other endurance athletes. It features motivational messages, tips and techniques for training and racing, and interviews with athletes and coaches.

Grape Radio

http://graperadio.com/wp-rss2.php

Discussion about all things related to wine. Whether you're an oenophile of long standing or you're just learning the rules about reds and whites, you'll find something interesting and edifying in this podcast.

Coverville

http://www.coverville.com/index.xml

A fully licensed, high-quality music podcast that features cover versions of songs that are interesting, arcane, unusual, or otherwise collected from somewhere off the beaten path.

MacCast

http://feeds.feedburner.com/maccast

This podcast is hosted by Adam Christianson and bills itself as "For Mac Geeks, By Mac Geeks." What more is there to say? Other than the fact that, unlike *Inside Mac Radio*, this program is conceived and created as a true podcast, not re-purposed radio content.

Marlaina By Ear

http://www.blindcast.com/podcast/blindspot.html (*blog address*)

Marlaina Lieberg is blind. A few years ago, a long-time interest in audio led her into the world of web-based radio. Podcasting has proved to be a natural next step. Every day, Marlaina and some of her colleagues demonstrate the potential of podcasting to build diverse communities of interest. This podcast for the blind community is an extraordinary example.

The Beatles Chronicles

http://feeds.feedburner.com/typepad/arYY

If you're a Beatles fan (and, really, who isn't?), this is an absolutely amazing collection of music and interview clips from The Fab Four. You might wonder if a 10-hour series about one band might get a little tedious after a while, even if it is the greatest rock band ever. The answer is: No. (As Dr. Winston O'Boogie once said, "You should have been there.")

Battlestar Galactica

http://www.scifi.com/battlestar/downloads/podcast/podcast.xml

Exclusive commentary on each episode of the Sci-Fi Channel series by the show's executive producer, Ronald D. Moore. If you think about the "Director's Commentary" feature on some of your DVDs, you'll have a great idea of what this podcast is all about. Be careful, though. This podcast is designed to be listened to during each episode. If you listen to it before you watch an episode, it might spoil any surprises the episode might contain!

How To Do Stuff

http://tmaffin.libsyn.com/rss

An eclectic collection of audio essays on how to do things. You might not feel as though you need pointers on "How to Wash Your Face Properly," but "How to Do a Killer Card Trick" is probably a something that might come in useful every once in a while.

Engadget

http://media.weblogsinc.com/common/videos/pt/rss.xml

News and info about gadgets. Big gadgets. Small gadgets. Expensive gadgets. High-tech gadgets. Useful gadgets. Extravagant gadgets. You get the idea.

The Bitterest Pill

http://www.danklass.com/pill/pill.xml

Dan Klass is a stay-at-home dad, an actor, and a comedian. At the very least, this podcast will give you some ideas about what to do with your time if you don't have to be in an office all day long. And, who knows? You might find it funny, too.

Autoblog

http://podcasts.autoblog.com/rss.xml

The Autoblog podcast is a relatively recent extension of an established blog about cars and the auto industry. If you share the quintessentially American passion for cars—including ones from Germany, Japan, Sweden, and Korea—then this podcast is guaranteed to get your motor running.

iTUNEs

The most influential company in the digital music industry is staking out some turf in the podcasting market, impacting podcast consumers as well as podcast producers.

Introducing iTunes 4.9

In July of 2005, Apple fired the shot heard around the podcasting world when it introduced Version 4.9 of its popular iTunes software. That new version of iTunes became the first mainstream music management software to incorporate support for podcasting. (Podcasting support remains an integral part of iTunes with the release of iTunes 5.01, the most current version of the software as this book goes to press.)

The significance of the iTunes announcement for podcasters can hardly be over-stated. Apple legitimized podcasting, transforming it instantly from an intriguing technological curiosity into a mainstream medium. More importantly, it exposes podcasting to an audience that is orders of magnitude larger than ever before. Apple dominates the market for portable music players with its line of iPod players. In fact, most estimates of Apple's share of the market list it at approximately 70 percent, with its line of iPod players, and every single one of those iPod owners is using iTunes.

For the purposes of navigation, iTunes treats podcasting as a cross between an audio book and its own musical genre. On the iTunes home page, you can navigate to the main podcast page from the Choose Store column on the left side of the page, as shown in Figure D.1.

FIGURE D.1

Start exploring iTunes podcasts by selecting Podcasts from the Chose Store column on the left. (You can also select Podcasts from the Choose Genre pull-down menu.

That selection will take you to iTunes Podcasting home page. From there, you can browse through thousands of podcasts to find and subscribe to the ones you're interested in.

When the history of podcasting is written, the iTunes announcement will be seen as the new medium's first watershed event. While the sheer number of iTunes users is an important element in making this a milestone, it is certainly not the only one.

iTunes Offers One-Click Subscriptions

Apart from exposing podcasting to many, many more potential listeners, Apple also enhanced the user experience dramatically. The most important element of this transformation is the introduction of single-click subscriptions to podcasts. While the technological cognoscenti were able to navigate through the multi-step process of subscribing to a podcast, the average user often found the experience a bit intimidating. (If you refer to Chapter 1, "An Overview of Podcasting," you'll see what we mean!)

Once you find a podcast you're interested in, iTunes reduces the subscription process to a simple single click of your mouse, as shown in Figure D.2.

FIGURE D.2

Clicking the Subscribe button is all you need to do to begin you podcast subscription in iTunes.

Just like dedicated podcatching software, iTunes allows you to manage the settings for your subscription. Podcast settings are accessed by a Settings button at the bottom of the iTunes window, allowing you to control how iTunes handles your podcast subscriptions, as shown in Figure D.3.

FIGURE D.3

iTunes allows you to specify how you want the software to handle your podcasts.

iTunes Allows Listeners to Manage Music and Podcasts from a Single Application

Prior to the release of iTunes 4.9, listeners needed to manage their podcast subscriptions with whichever podcatching software they were using, then import their podcasts into iTunes, a process that was not always seamless or thoroughly reliable. iTunes now allows listeners to manage their podcasts and subscriptions from a single interface, improving reliability and enhancing ease of use.

Eliminating the need for multiple applications to manage podcasts and podcast subscriptions raises the ease-of-use bar dramatically for the entire podcasting industry.

Getting Your Podcast into the iTunes Directory

Fortunately, Apple made it simple for you to use iTunes as a vehicle for distributing your podcast. In fact, submitting a podcast to iTunes is almost as easy as subscribing to one.

From the main Podcast page on iTunes, simply select the Submit a Podcast link on the left side of the page. From there, iTunes will guide you through a series of steps that will allow you to submit your podcast to the iTunes directory, as shown in Figure D.4.

FIGURE D.4

iTunes guides you through the steps you need to follow in order to submit your podcast.

You'll need an iTunes account to submit your podcast, something you already have if you're an iTunes user. Once your podcast has been submitted, it will take a few days for it to appear in the iTunes directory.

The Good News and the Bad News

There's no question about the fact that iTunes makes it easier than ever before for large numbers of listeners to find and subscribe to your podcast. It significantly reduces the technological barrier between you and your listeners. That's the good news.

The bad news is that iTunes is not particularly geared toward supporting independent podcasts. Its slant is more toward podcasts from large media outlets, primarily radio content that has been re-purposed into podcast format.

Another problem with iTunes is the fact that, while it makes it easier for the 70 percent of the market that uses iPods, it does not allow you to reach the 30 percent of the market that doesn't. While Apple's share of the MP3 player market remains high, that isn't a big issue. If non-iPod players ever start to erode Apple's market share, however, the dynamics of the situation will begin to change.

Finally, you should be aware of the fact that Apple has chosen to use an RSS implementation that is slightly non-standard. If you use a third-party application or service such as FeedBurner or Feeder to generate your RSS feed, chances are that it's been updated to accomodate iTunes. If you're generating your own RSS feed, then you need to make sure it conforms to Apple's technical specifications for the feed. The current technical specs can be found here:

http://phobos.apple.com/static/iTunesRSS.html

The Bottom Line

iTunes is a terrific place to list your podcast, and its support for podcasting is certainly a great thing for podcasting, in general. It's important, however, to keep iTunes in perspective and don't rely on it as the exclusive vehicle for your podcast.

Index

X – Y – Z

Other Related Titles

White Collar Slacker's Handbook
Marc Saltzman
0-7897-3310-2
$14.99 US /
$19.99 CAN

Absolute Beginner's Guide to Security, Spam, Spyware & Viruses
Andy Walker
0-7897-3459-1
$21.99 US /
$29.99 CAN

Absolute Beginner's Guide to eBay, Third Edition
Michael Miller
0-7897-3431-1
$19.99 US /
$27.99 CAN

The MacAddict Guide to Making Music with GarageBand
Jay Shaffer and Gary Rosenzweig
0-7897-3226-2
$24.99 US /
$35.99 CAN

Mobile Guide to BlackBerry
Bill Foust
0-7897-3343-9
$24.99 US /
$34.99 CAN

Anywhere Computing with Laptops: Making Mobile Easier
Harold Davis
0-7897-3327-7
$24.99 US /
$34.99 CAN

Upgrading and Repairing PCs, 16th Edition
Scott Mueller
0-7897-3173-8
$59.99 US /
$86.99 CAN

Absolute Beginner's Guide to Home Networking
Mark Edward Soper
0-7897-3205-X
$18.95 US /
$26.95 CAN

Treo Essentials
Michael Morrison
0-7897-3328-5
$24.99 US /
$34.99 CAN /

iPod and iTunes Starter Kit, 2nd Edition
Brad Miser and Tim Robertson
0-7897-3463-X (USA)
0-7897-3464-8 (International)
$34.99 US /
$48.99 CAN

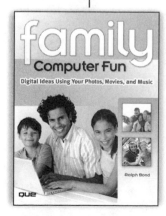

Family Computer Fun: Digital Ideas Using Your Photos, Movies, and Music
Ralph Bond
0-7897-3378-1
$24.99 US /
$29.99 CAN

www.quepublishing.com

All prices are subject to change.

Check the Web for More Podcasting Goodies!

Absolute Beginner's Guide to Podcasting gives you the skills you need to create your own podcast. You can get more goodies at Que Publishing's podcasting page.

At www.quepublishing.com/podcasting you'll find:

- Links to the authors' podcast
- News about the latest contests and promotions
- More podcasting resources
- The latest updates to *Absolute Beginner's Guide to Podcasting*
- Links to a wealth of articles and sample chapters on dozens of technology topics

http://www.quepublishing.com/podcasting